Charles & Diana

SOME MEMORIES
OF THE WEDDING

'I mostly remember when they came out of St Paul's Cathedral and the crowds were cheering.'

Alita Findon, 9 years old

'I felt sorry for the soldiers and the policemen and police ladies who had to look after the people cheering.'

Marijit Dass, 7 years old

'I liked the bit when they kissed each other. That made me feel sort of funny.'

Jamie Houghton, 5 years old

'I wish we could have another day like it.'

Teresa Walsh, 11 years old

ICH DIEN

Charles & Diana

Their story told by
JOHN CRAVEN
including children's memories
of the Royal Wedding

Research by Katie Griffiths

SPARROW
BOOKS

A Sparrow Book
Published by Arrow Books Limited
17–21 Conway Street, London W1P 6JD

An imprint of the Hutchinson Publishing Group

London Melbourne Sydney Auckland
Johannesburg and agencies
throughout the world

First published 1982
© Helpwell Ltd 1982

Set in Linotron Palatino by
Rowland Phototypesetting Limited
Bury St Edmunds, Suffolk

Made and printed in Great Britain
by The Anchor Press Ltd
Tiptree, Essex

ISBN 0 09 928790 0

Contents

Introduction

A royal engagement, a royal wedding, and a royal baby – all within two years, and all involving two much-loved people, Charles and Diana. Unlike almost any other young couple getting married, their romance has been followed with great interest by millions of people – because they could be the next king and queen.

When Charles, Prince of Wales, proposed marriage to Lady Diana Spencer, the news flashed across the world. Hundreds of television stations showed the pageantry of their wedding at St Paul's Cathedral in London. And the announcement a few months later that they were expecting a baby put the seal on a happy moment of history for everyone who admires and respects the British royal family.

In this book, I shall be telling the life stories of the Prince and Princess and remembering all the events surrounding their public lives together since they met, in Scotland, in the summer of 1980. There's space, too, for you to write down your memories of their wedding day – where you were, what you saw, and how and if you celebrated it. There's a page, too, for you to fill in the details of their baby.

So I hope that, when you've read the book and

completed your part of it, you'll put it somewhere safe and keep it as a reminder of a rather special time.

John Craven

I

The Courtship

The romance that led to what has been called 'the wedding of the century' began in Scotland in the summer of 1980. Prince Charles was staying at Balmoral, the royal family's holiday home on the banks of the river Dee. Lady Diana's sister, Lady Jane, was staying on the estate with her husband, Mr Robert Fellowes, the Queen's assistant private secretary, and Lady Diana went there to help her sister with her first baby.

Though many people imagine that Prince Charles and Lady Diana have known each other since childhood, neither of them can remember meeting before November 1977 – the year of the Queen's Silver Jubilee. 'I remember thinking what fun she was then – a splendid sixteen-year-old,' said Charles later.

But in July 1980, she caught the eye of the Prince of Wales. James Whittaker, who writes about the Royal Family for the *Daily Star* newspaper, claims to be the first journalist to have spotted the romance. He was snooping round the river Dee while Charles was fishing, and thought he saw something sparkling. It turned out to be a mirror held by Lady Diana which she was using to watch Whittaker and his photographer who were behind her.

Very calmly, she got up and walked away up the hill, without turning round so they could not get a photograph of her face.

Shortly afterwards, rumours of the romance were on every front page, and for the next six months reporters and photographers followed Diana wherever she went. They camped outside her flat, cornered her as she arrived at the kindergarten where she worked – one reporter even tried to get inside the kindergarten through the lavatory window!

She was photographed with some of the children and, though she didn't realize it, the skirt she was wearing was transparent. When she saw the pictures she was overcome with embarrassment, though Prince Charles apparently remarked later that her legs looked 'pretty damn good!'

Speculation grew in Fleet Street, the home of British newspapers, as the day of the Prince's thirty-second birthday drew near. Would this be a good time for the engagement to be announced? But the day passed, and nothing happened.

Then came a row over an interview in which Lady Diana was quoted as saying she would 'like to be married very soon'. She denied saying those words, and it seemed to many people that she was being hounded by the press. Her mother, Mrs Shand-Kydd, wrote to *The Times* protesting about the treatment Diana was getting from journalists, and asking if it was really fair. After all, Diana was just a member of the public – she didn't get any special protection from the Palace or the police.

In the House of Commons, sixty MPs from all parties joined in the protest at the way she was being

pestered. Debates were held on television programmes – but that just gave even more coverage to
the Lady Diana story. And the press did not go away.
Their readers, they said, wanted to know every possible scrap of information about the romance. One
photographer even disguised himself as a road-
sweeper, and sprang up to snap Lady Diana una-
wares.

Fleet Street had been looking for a bride for the
Prince of Wales for many years, and lots of 'possibles'
had been splashed across their pages. But this time it
seemed to be the real thing, and there was lots to go on
– Diana had visited the Prince at Highgrove and had
stayed with some of his friends.

But, unknown to the journalists, she had also se-
cretly gone back to Scotland later in the year. She
stayed at the Queen Mother's house, Birkhall, to be
near the Prince.

When New Year came, the press were treated to a
right royal game of hide-and-seek. They knew that
Lady Diana was with the royal family at Sandringham,
but none of them had actually seen her. There were so
many reporters and cameramen trampling around
that the Queen actually said: 'I wish you people would
go away.' And Prince Charles, keeping his sense of
humour, yelled out: 'A happy new year to you, but a
particularly nasty one to your editors!'

Through most of the hassle, Lady Diana came out
smiling, and many people think that perhaps the royal
family were putting her through a kind of test. If she
could survive this constant attention by the press and
still stay the shy, charming girl that not only the Prince
but the world had fallen in love with, then she would

indeed be a worthy wife for the heir to the throne. Diana passed the test with flying colours.

I remember one particular incident when the television news cameras were filming her getting into her new Mini Metro. Reporters tried to make her speak to them but she wouldn't. She smiled and muttered sweetly but refused to be drawn by any of the questions. She was getting the kind of treatment that some film-stars pray for, and she obviously didn't want it. But she remained good-humoured and very polite, and looked so beautiful.

In January, Charles and Diana had a rendezvous at dawn on the Berkshire Downs, at the Lambourn stables of his racehorse trainer, Nick Gaselee. The press arrived a couple of hours later and took pictures of their empty cars parked nose-to-nose.

There were more meetings at Highgrove before Charles set off on a skiing holiday. When he returned, they met again at Highgrove – in fact, Diana drove hundreds of miles in her Metro during their courtship to see Charles.

In February, Diana flew to Australia to see her mother and get away from all the publicity. For a long time no one knew where she was. Mrs Shand-Kydd told the press that her daughter was not with her – she even said they had got the wrong continent!

Later, she was totally unashamed about having lied to protect Diana. She said her daughter needed to get away, and so strict was the secrecy in Australia that even the Prince had difficulty getting through by phone on a couple of occasions – his calls were thought to be hoaxes!

What no one except close friends and relatives knew

was that, just before Diana left for Australia in February, Charles had proposed to her. They had been having dinner together in the sitting room of his private apartment in Buckingham Palace when he asked her to marry him.

In an interview later, Charles explained: 'I wanted to give her a chance to think about it – to think if it was all going to be too awful.'

And Lady Diana chipped in: 'Oh, I never had any doubts about it.'

Then came the big scoop! *The Times* announced on the morning of 23 February that the engagement would be made official later that day. So the most sedate of Britain's newspapers, the one least likely to have been pursuing Lady Diana, got the big story. The editor remained silent about who told him the news.

The announcement was made that morning while the Queen was presenting honours at an investiture ceremony at Buckingham Palace. The Lord Chamberlain stepped forward and read the following statement:

'It is with great pleasure that the Queen and the Duke of Edinburgh announce the betrothal of their beloved son, the Prince of Wales, to the Lady Diana Spencer, daughter of the Earl Spencer and the Honourable Mrs Shand-Kydd.'

Crowds immediately began to gather outside the Palace, and the band of the Coldstream Guards played 'Congratulations'.

Now there was no more need for all the secrecy, and in the afternoon Prince Charles and his fiancée walked in the Palace grounds, posing for photographers. Those pictures have already become part of history.

Diana showed off her engagement ring – an oval sapphire surrounded by fourteen diamonds and set in 18-carat white gold. It came from one of the royal jewellers, Garrards, and it's estimated to have cost about £30,000.

It was a chilly day, and Diana's fingers looked a little blue from the cold. She was wearing a now much-copied blue suit with a blue and white blouse, and flat shoes so that she wouldn't seem taller than the Prince – she is 5 foot 10 inches, and he is 5 foot 11 inches.

Among the crowds thronging the Palace gates were Diana's father and step-mother, the Earl and Countess Spencer. The Earl had his camera and told reporters: 'I have photographed every event in my daughter's life, and I am not going to miss this one.'

The Prince had telephoned him the previous week and said: 'Can I marry your daughter? I have asked her and, very surprisingly, she said yes!'

Then the Earl chuckled, wondering what would have happened if he had said no.

News of the engagement was flashed round the world. Prince Charles's previous command, HMS *Bronington*, fired a 21-gun salute at Plymouth.

Telegrams of congratulation began flooding in. Luckily, the Palace staff had a few hours' warning – they knew something was about to happen when they found the fridges crammed with bottles of champagne!

Prince Charles said he was 'positively delighted and frankly amazed that Diana is prepared to take me on'. And the whole nation was delighted along with him.

In an interview, Charles and Diana talked about the things they had in common. Both love the countryside, and he would like to spend much more time there.

Said Diana: 'We both love music and dancing, and we both have the same sense of humour.'

'You'll definitely need that,' said the Prince with a laugh.

Perhaps the only interest they don't have in common is a love of horse riding. 'I fell off a horse and lost my nerve,' confided Diana.

On the night of the engagement, the couple faced the television cameras, and Diana let Charles do most of the talking. Her first impression of Charles? 'Pretty amazing!' At the end of the interview, they were asked if they were in love. 'Of course,' answered Diana immediately.

'Whatever that means,' smiled Charles.

Then the two of them had dinner with the Queen Mother and Diana's grandmother, Ruth, Lady Fermoy, at Clarence House – the Queen Mother's home just down The Mall from Buckingham Palace. Lady Fermoy is one of the Queen Mother's ladies-in-waiting and a great friend. Clarence House was to become Diana's home until the day of the wedding. The Queen Mother was the ideal person to help Diana understand and master all the special duties of the royal family.

Suddenly, Lady Diana's status had changed. She was no longer just a member of the public. Detectives guarded her now, and she was to be groomed for a job she could never have dreamed of a few months before – a future queen of England.

Diana had to move out of the London flat she had shared with the three friends who had helped her during those trying months with the press, and who had kept her greatest secret.

Later, they told of how they first learned that their close friend was going to be a Princess. Virginia Pitman said: 'Di just sat on the bed next to me and said she was going to marry Prince Charles.'

Carolyn Pride was in the loo at the time. 'Lady Diana told me through the door.'

They all began to shriek with excitement, and then cried with happiness.

The flatmates got a lot of praise for keeping the secret so well. Throughout the courtship, they knew what was going on but told no one. They saw when flowers or other gifts arrived for Diana from Charles, and in the early days she used to joke that she was going out with Charlie Renfrew (Baron Renfrew is one of Charles's titles).

The morning after the engagement, it took Diana just twenty minutes to pack her things from the flat, while two policemen waited outside to escort her back to Clarence House. She had breakfast with the Queen Mother before opening thousands of goodwill telegrams. Her new life had begun.

2
The Prince's Story

Charles Philip Arthur George, Prince of Wales, Duke of Cornwall, Earl of Chester, Duke of Rothesay, Earl of Carrick, Baron Renfrew, Lord of the Isles and Great Steward of Scotland, Knight of the Most Noble Order of the Garter, Knight of the Most Ancient and Most Noble Order of the Thistle, Grand Master and Principal Knight Grand Cross of the Most Honourable Order of the Bath, was once reported to have said: 'Boy, the things I do for England!'

At the time, he was visiting a jungle-survival school in Hong Kong, and at the invitation of some Gurkha soldiers, he was tasting curried snake-meat! It was all in the line of duty for the daring, dashing Prince whose great sense of fun has helped him in a lot of tight spots.

He seems to be an amazingly normal sort of person, which is quite an achievement for someone who's lived all his life amongst publicity and pageantry, and who has been destined to be King since the moment he was born, on 14 November 1948.

Prince Charles came into the world at a bleak time for Britain. The country was still recovering from the effects of the Second World War, which had ended three years before. Things like new clothes, food and sweets were in short supply and, to add to the problems, the year before had seen one of the harshest ever winters.

So the arrival of a Prince cheered everyone up. The baby's mother, Princess Elizabeth, and her sister, Princess Margaret, were the daughters of King George the Sixth and Queen Elizabeth. As there were no sons Princess Elizabeth, the elder daughter, would be the next monarch.

A year earlier, she had married Prince Philip, and their first son was born at Buckingham Palace. Crowds gathered to see the announcement of his birth posted on the Palace gates, and the water in the fountains of Trafalgar Square was turned blue for a boy.

The bells of Westminster Abbey and St Paul's Cathedral pealed out the news, and there were flags and bunting everywhere. At his christening, he wore a robe that had been worn by all of Queen Victoria's children a century before, and by his mother and his aunt Margaret at their christenings.

The baby prince and his parents lived at Clarence House, one of the royal residences in London, and he was looked after by two nannies. His sister, Anne, was born on 15 August 1950.

It wasn't long before he had his first taste of public adoration, though he was too young to realize it. The nannies used to take the two babies for walks in their prams through one of the London parks every day. But they started to attract so much attention that the walks were switched to parks further away, at Richmond and Wimbledon.

From the time he was old enough to walk, young

Charles was taught to bow to his great grandmother, Queen Mary, and he was also made to stand still for long periods. Training to be royal started early, and Princess Elizabeth and Prince Philip made sure Anne and Charles understood and appreciated the advantages they had, and were careful not to spoil them.

Princess Elizabeth was spending more and more time standing in for her father, King George, at official engagements. He was a sick man and in February 1952, while Elizabeth and Philip were on a visit to the African country of Kenya, he died. She flew home to Britain as Queen Elizabeth the Second.

With her family, she moved to Buckingham Palace and her Coronation in the following June was a glorious state occasion. Prince Charles, as the Duke of Cornwall, should have sworn an oath of allegiance to his mother the Queen. But it was decided that he was too young to participate in the ceremony, although he did watch with his grandmother, who had become Queen Elizabeth, the Queen Mother.

In their new nursery at the Palace, Charles and Anne had found lots of their familiar toys, and there are reports that Charles used to run down the corridors with the corgis beating an old saucepan with a wooden spoon. But there was discipline, too. He was punished for putting an ice-cube down a footman's neck, and for sticking his tongue out at a crowd.

Everyone at the Palace called the youngsters simply Charles and Anne – no titles! – and they didn't have to bow or curtsey to the Queen.

Prince Charles had his own private governess, Miss Peebles, who was known as Mispy. Apparently, he had trouble with arithmetic – who doesn't! – but geography was easier because Mispy showed him the routes his parents had taken on their tours around the world.

The Queen wanted her children to go to school like other children, instead of being taught at home as royal youngsters had always been before. Yet she was troubled by the way Charles and Anne were followed by the press when they made educational trips to places of interest. So a request was made to all the editors of newspapers to cut down their 'coverage' of the children – and this seemed to work, at least for a while.

Prince Charles went to a preparatory school in London called Hill House, at first just going to afternoon sessions on the playing fields while continuing his lessons with Mispy in the mornings. The following term, he went to Hill House full time and on his first day had lessons, then a lunch of beef and carrots, and in the afternoon did a painting of Tower Bridge. Millions of newspaper readers in many countries got all the details – never in history had a child's first day at school caused so much interest.

For Charles, going to school meant many new things – it was the first time he'd handled money, bought his own sweets and travelled on a bus. His first school report was satisfactory – average in most things, except arithmetic!

For his next school, the Queen and Prince Philip chose Cheam, a private boarding school where Prince Philip had once been a pupil. The Queen went to inspect the school and introduce her son to the headmasters, Peter Beck and Mark Wheeler. She noted the hard beds in the dormitory and said: 'Well, you won't be able to bounce on these!'

He started there when he was eight and quickly fell into the daily routine of boarding school: up at 7.15 and, after washing and dressing, inspection by the matron; then filing in to prayers and shaking hands with one of the headmasters; at meals, all boys took it in turns to wait on each other; lessons from nine till one, with a break for a glass of milk and a bun. Wednesdays and Saturdays were half holidays and on the other afternoons the boys could play games and learn art and handicrafts. High tea was at six o'clock and bedtime was seven except on Sunday nights when they were allowed to stay up and watch a film.

According to newspaper stories of the time, it was Charles's love of sweets which helped him break down some of the awkward barriers between himself and other boys. One story, printed but said to be untrue, was that Charles had to auction some of his belongings to get enough money to buy sweets – the Queen wasn't giving him enough pocket money. When the story appeared in American newspapers, the Association of Retail Confectioners there quickly sent him a parcel of assorted sweets – and they were shared round the school!

It still worried the royal family that Charles was getting far too much attention from the press, with cameramen lurking in the bushes round the school hoping to get pictures of him. Once again, the Queen's Press Secretary, Richard Colville, called newspaper editors to Buckingham Palace. The message was clear: leave the Prince alone.

Charles joined in lots of activities at Cheam – including carpentry, pottery, woodcraft, outdoor cooking and wildlife studies. He was said to be of higher-than-average intelligence, but only managed to get average results. He was very good at English, but maths was still giving him problems!

Charles watched the opening of the Commonwealth Games in Cardiff on television, and he heard a recording of the Queen's speech – she was unable to attend in person – in which she said: 'I intend to make my son, Charles, Prince of Wales today.' According to reports, it was the first that he had heard of it!

The Prince started piano lessons and sang in the school choir and in the local church, St Peter's in Headley. He was noted for being considerate to others, and after games of rugby was sometimes heard apologizing to other players for trampling on them. But he didn't really enjoy rugby or cricket, though he quite liked football. In his final year at Cheam, he captained the First Eleven soccer team – but they lost every match!

Some of his other interests, such as shooting and fishing, he developed during the school holidays – he was taught to fish by his grandmother, the Queen Mother, who is a very keen and skilled angler. And before he was thirteen, he'd been taught to drive a car by his father on the private roads of their estates.

Whenever the Queen and Prince Philip visited Cheam School, they wanted to be treated as ordinary parents with no special privileges. And while at the school, Charles discovered a love for acting which has stayed with him. He played the title role in a school production of Shakespeare's *Richard III* after the boy who was due to take the part went sick. It was on the day of that performance, on 19 February 1962, that a headmaster announced the birth of Charles's younger brother, Prince Andrew.

In 1962, when he was thirteen, it was time for Charles to move to a secondary school, and the choice was Gordonstoun – another of his father's old schools. The aim there was to teach drive and leadership, with the emphasis on service to others and physical activities.

The school was at Morayshire in Scotland, and conditions were pretty bleak – the boys lived in single-storey huts with bare floors, no paint on the walls, and light bulbs without any shades. Pupils wore short trousers, and took cold showers twice a day.

'It may have been a bit tougher than other schools,' said Charles later. 'I mean it was not very nice getting up at ten to seven in the morning in the winter in the pitch dark and running about in shorts and nothing else but a pair of gym shoes. But you only ran a matter of a hundred yards, then got under a hot shower and then a cold shower. You did not have cold showers by themselves. It was quite a harsh regime in a way, but it does do a great deal for one's character.'

At first, he didn't seem to enjoy Gordonstoun very much and visited his grandmother at Balmoral as often as he could. But eventually he got into the swing of it and became particularly good at swimming and canoeing. Once he was on a canoeing expedition that got very hairy when a storm blew up.

In his second year he joined the Junior Training Plan – a scheme which gave him a wider choice of activities. One of them was a cruise on the school yacht, *Pinta*.

On 17 June 1963, the *Pinta* sailed into Stornoway on the Isle of Lewis – and that led to 'the Cherry Brandy Incident', a story which made world headlines.

The boys were allowed ashore at lunchtime, and told they could go to the cinema in the afternoon. They were left at the Crown Hotel, and word quickly got round that Prince Charles was amongst the party.

Trying to get away from all the people who'd gathered to goggle at him, Charles slipped into another room of the hotel which happened to be a bar. Perhaps it was because everyone else there was drinking that Charles thought he would be less obvious if he, too, was enjoying a quiet drink. So the Prince, for whatever his reasons, ordered a cherry brandy. Unluckily for him, a freelance reporter happened to be around and spotted his illegal drink – at fourteen he was much too young to be sipping alcohol in bars. Next day, the story was in all the papers, and Charles was punished at school by being demoted from the Junior Training Plan. But he managed to get his place back quite quickly.

He passed his O-level examinations in five subjects – Latin, history, English language, English literature and French. He failed physics – and maths! It took him another eighteen months to pass maths, and he gave up physics. During his last year at Gordonstoun, he played the trumpet in the school orchestra and acted the lead part in a production of *Macbeth*. He was also a prefect, known at Gordonstoun as a colour-bearer.

In 1965, he began to accompany his parents more and more on their official duties. He attended the funeral of Britain's great wartime Prime Minister, Sir Winston

Churchill, and as Duke of Cornwall met a committee that looked after all the lands and property belonging to him.

Though he had a good time at Gordonstoun, Prince Charles wanted a break, so for a while he really got away – to Australia. He became a pupil at Geelong Church of England Grammar School, but instead of attending the main school in Melbourne, he went to its outward-bound section on the slopes of Mount Timbertop.

The 135 boys at Timbertop did a minimum of school-work and a maximum of 'survival techniques'. They did exploring, hiking and fishing. The boys chopped their own firewood, raised their own farm animals and looked after their own homesteads. Charles enjoyed himself so much that when his term was over, he asked to stay for another one. . . . His experiences there were making him more self-confident.

This showed while he was on his way home when the aircraft had to stop at Brisbane for refuelling. Someone told him that he ought to step out and say a few words to the people who'd gathered to see him. He felt very nervous, but as he walked over to them he felt 'something click inside' . . . and he says since then he has never felt awkward in public.

The time at Timbertop had been a marvellous break, but now it was back to Gordonstoun and work for his A-level examinations. When he returned, he found that his fellow pupils in Windmill Lodge – his 'house' – had voted him helper, or head of house. And in his last two terms, he became guardian – the head boy, and passed his A-levels in history and French.

Though schooldays were over, Prince Charles went on, in October 1967, to university – to Trinity College, Cambridge, where he studied archeology and social anthropology. He had only two special privileges which set him apart from all the other students: a kitchen was fitted so he could eat in his room instead of in the dining hall, and he also had his own telephone.

Charles was under tremendous pressure to do well, not only because his teaching was taking place in public, as it were, but also because other students had protested about what they thought was the unfair way he'd got to Cambridge. He had only two average A-levels, while standards for others who hoped to get there, they said, were much higher.

He studied hard, and in the evenings had meetings lasting forty-five minutes with Lord Butler, the master of the college. Lord Butler had been a famous Conservative politician – serving as Deputy Prime Minister, Home Secretary, and Chancellor of the Exchequer – and their meetings no doubt helped to satisfy Charles's curiosity about many subjects, including politics.

During his second term, he was asked to write for the university magazine, *Varsity*. He agreed, and in his article mentioned a dustman who sang outside his window – and woke him up! The dustman was hunted down and offered a recording contract, and for a short time became a bit of a celebrity. And from then on, the rubbish collection outside the Prince's window was delayed until nine o'clock!

Charles also became a great success taking part in light-hearted college revues on the stage – and he included the singing dustman in one of his sketches.

At the end of the first year, he did well in exams, but decided to switch his studies to history.

In 1969, Prince Charles spent a term at the University College of Wales in Aberystwyth studying the Welsh language as part of his preparations for the day when he truly became the Prince of Wales. It's a difficult language to learn, and he went there amid protests from Welsh Nationalists. There were many demonstrations, and security had to be tightened.

But Charles coped well right from the start by speaking to local people in the few words of Welsh he already knew. After eight weeks of intensive study came the big test – he made a speech to the Welsh League of Youth fluently, without a single mistake. This so impressed everyone in Wales that many of those who had feelings against him found them disappearing.

The Investiture of the Prince of Wales dates back to the time many centuries ago when King Edward the First presented his infant son to the Welsh barons at Caernarvon. The last time an investiture had been held was for Charles's great-uncle, later King Edward the Eighth. The ceremony took place at Caernarvon and reportedly the Prince had not enjoyed it at all – nor the uniform he'd had to wear.

This time the Queen was determined that the cost of the occasion should be kept as low as possible, even though preparations began twenty months beforehand, overseen by the Duke of Norfolk. Lord Snowdon, who was then married to Princess Margaret, was chosen to supervise the staging of the ceremony at Caernarvon Castle. Among his ideas was a canopy made from perspex supported by steel poles which looked like lances – modern yet with a medieval look, and very practical should it rain.

In the run-up to the event, there was a bombing campaign by a small group of extremists, and a hoax bomb was found along the railway track that the royal train was using on its journey into Wales. But public opinion in Wales had been growing ever stronger in the Prince's favour, helped no doubt by a remarkable film on television called 'Royal Family'. For the first time, TV cameras had been allowed to go 'backstage' in the royal household and film members of the family relaxing together.

When the time came, even the mayor of Caernarvon – who'd been unmoved by all the fuss of the preparations – called the twenty-year-old Prince 'the ace in the royal pack'.

For the ceremony, on 1 July 1969, Charles was dressed in the uniform of the colonel-in-chief of the newly created Royal Regiment of Wales. He entered the castle flanked by the Secretary of State for Wales, the Wales Herald Extraordinary and two peers. Behind, five Welsh peers carried the insignia of the Investiture – a silver-gilt sword, a golden rod symbolizing the Prince's authority, a ring symbolizing his 'marriage' to the country, a mantle of purple silk velvet and ermine, and a coronet.

The ceremony, in which the Prince swore an oath of allegiance to The Queen, was conducted in both Welsh and English. Ten thousand people were in the castle to witness the pageantry, and five hundred million people saw it on television.

Afterwards came a four-day tour of Wales, with

cheering crowds wherever he went. The Investiture had been a great success in every way.

In that same year of 1969, his twenty-first birthday was celebrated with a lavish party at Buckingham Palace for 400 guests. There was music from the famous violinist Yehudi Menuhin and the Bath Festival Orchestra. Later in the evening came music of a different kind, from the Prince's favourite pop singers, The Three Degrees.

At Easter 1970, he joined the royal tour of Australia and New Zealand, and then went on to visit Japan on his own, dining with Emperor Hirohito. While visiting the Sony electronics company there, he learnt they wanted to start a factory somewhere in Europe. He urged the top man to think about building the factory in Wales. Four years later, the Prince opened the new Sony factory in Glamorgan – a good example of the way that Charles cares for the country that he 'married' in that magnificent ceremony at Caernarvon.

It was a busy time for him, and perhaps because of all the interruptions for royal duties, Charles didn't leave Cambridge with a sparkling degree. He got what's called a lower second – a good, solid achievement.

While he was still at Cambridge, Charles began learning to fly, and after university he started on the first part of his training with the armed services by joining a course at Cranwell, the RAF's flying college. Charles didn't want to miss any part of the course, and despite all the anxiety about an heir to the throne flinging himself out of aeroplanes, he was determined he should parachute. After lessons on the ground, he jumped from the plane and landed safely with only one minor hitch when his feet got caught in the rigging lines of the parachute.

Always a man for jokes, on April Fool's Day at Cranwell he arranged for an announcement to be made that the firm which makes the RAF's footwear had discovered a fault in the heels and 'could everyone please bring their shoes to the porter's lodge'!

He passed out of Cranwell on 20 August 1971, and his report stated that he would make 'an excellent fighter pilot at supersonic speeds'.

Then, following several of his royal forebears, he went into the Navy, joining the Royal Naval College at Dartmouth on a course for university graduates. After long hours in the classroom learning about seamanship and navigation, he did a spell on board the guided missile destroyer HMS *Norfolk* and took part in fleet exercises in the Mediterranean. He also did submarine training, including emergency escapes without any kind of breathing apparatus.

Later, he joined HMS *Minerva*, and when she sailed to the Caribbean Charles was both an officer and a royal ambassador. He left *Minerva* in September 1973, for a period of royal duties, and in January 1974 he flew to Singapore to join HMS *Jupiter* as communications officer.

During a voyage through the waters of the Far East, fellow officers were allowed to behave with much more ease towards their royal colleague than might be expected, and Charles used to joke that he would send them to the Tower. When *Jupiter* docked at Plymouth, a black minibus was standing on the quayside with these words in gold lettering on its side: 'HMS Tower of London for officers of HMS *Jupiter*' – another of Charles's pranks!

While on board *Jupiter*, the Prince had become fascinated by the role of helicopters on warships. Shortly afterwards, he went on a three-month course at the Royal Naval air station at Yeovilton in Somerset, where he learnt to fly large twin-engined Wessex helicopters in all kinds of conditions, such as landing on the top of Mount Snowdon. Once one of his engines caught fire and he had to make an emergency landing in a field. At the end of the course, he was awarded the double-diamond trophy for the pilot who had made the most progress, and in the Fleet Air Arm he found his ideal branch of the armed services where he could mix his love of the sea with his love of flying. He joined the commando-carrying ship HMS *Hermes* with the Red Dragon flight of helicopters.

More royal duties followed, including a tour of Canada where among other things he dived beneath the ice to look at marine life in freezing waters, and then he returned to the Navy, to take command of the minesweeper HMS *Bronington*.

He made a fine captain of a great little ship, which rolled around in the waves quite alarmingly. When he left at the end of his command the crew in fine naval tradition pushed him ashore in a wheelchair decorated with a black lavatory seat – to remind him of his duties to the 'throne'.

Those duties were treated much more seriously when, during his mother's Silver Jubilee celebrations in 1977, he launched an appeal to help young people 'who felt aimless'. A year before he had set up the Prince's Trust, with the idea of 'enabling young people to find adventure, excitement and achievement by carrying through their own enterprises which contribute to their own and other people's development'. Prince Charles carried forward the ideals of the trust when he launched the Silver Jubilee Appeal, and within a year £16 million pounds had been raised.

As chairman, Charles has taken an active interest in any groups who've received help from the fund. And he was patron of an expedition called 'Operation Drake' in which a number of crews of people under the age of twenty-five took a 150-ton sailing ship round the world, following the route of Sir Francis Drake in the days of the first Queen Elizabeth. He himself sponsored one of the 200 young people who took part, and when the ship's engine needed replacing, he paid for nearly half of it.

Now that he has finished his life in the armed services, the Prince spends a lot of his time when he is not on royal duties running the Duchy of Cornwall, which is his main source of income. The Duchy dates back to 1337, when the title was created by King Edward the Third, and today it owns about 130,000 acres of land, including the Isles of Scilly and the Oval cricket ground in London. The Prince is probably one of the richest land-owners in the country, but half the money he earns from it was given to the government before his marriage.

During August Bank Holiday in 1979, the royal family faced a great tragedy. Lord Mountbatten was killed by a terrorist bomb while on holiday in Ireland.

Charles had had a very special friendship with his

BABYHOOD: Four months old, and Prince Charles plays with his mother's necklace in the first informal photograph taken of Princess Elizabeth and her son.
Lady Diana Spencer about to crawl off a rug in a picture from the family album snapped at Park House, Sandringham, on her first birthday.

*EARLY FORMS OF
TRANSPORT:* Toddler Diana
pushes a pram at Park House;
Charles takes his hands off the
wheel of his toy car to show
the Queen a fluffy white glove
puppet. The picture was taken
at Balmoral to mark his fourth
birthday in 1952.

MONKEYING AROUND:
Charles, in smart sailor suit,
makes friends with one of the
famous apes on the Rock of
Gibraltar.
Diana learning to play croquet
while on holiday at Itchenor,
West Sussex.

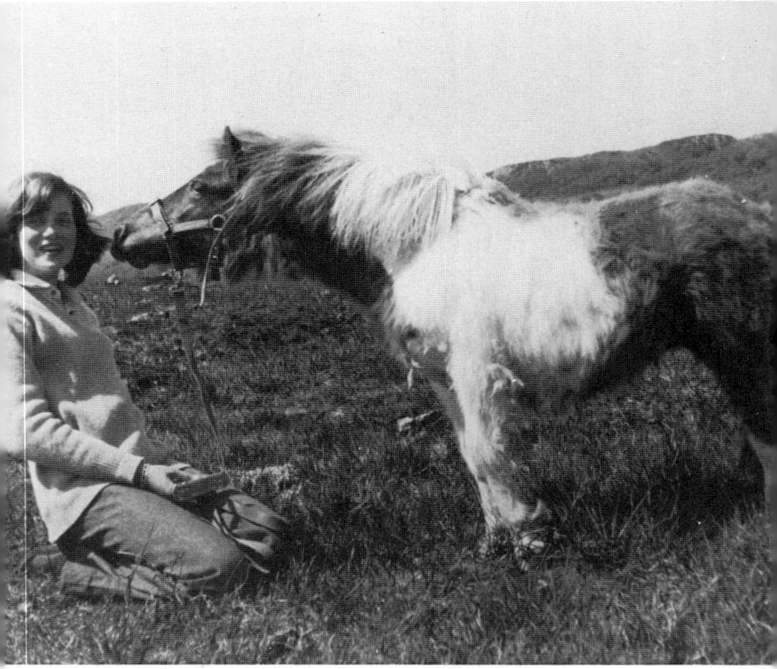
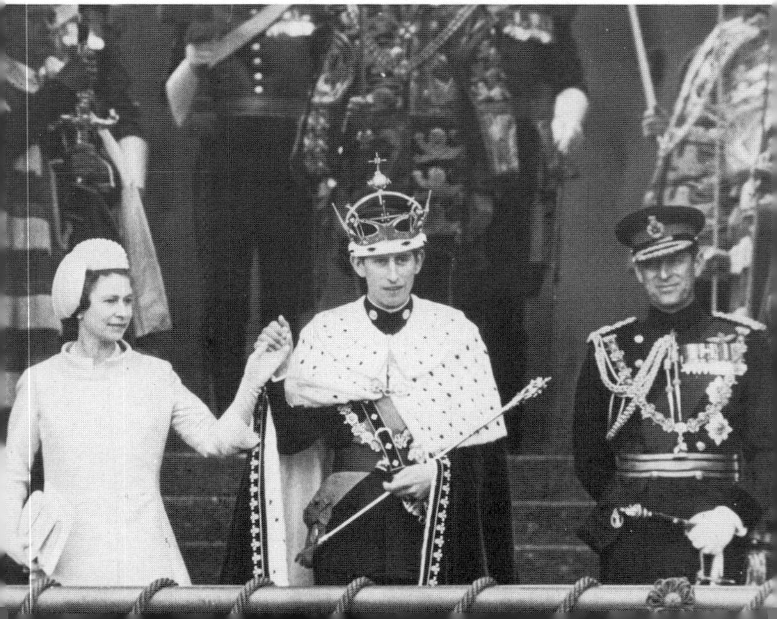

PALS!: A snuggle from a Shetland pony called Souffle for Diana at her mother's home in Scotland during the summer of 1974.

BEHOLD THE PRINCE!: The Queen presents her son the Prince of Wales to the people of Wales from the battlements of Caernarvon Castle during the Investiture ceremony in 1969.

FIRST FLIGHT: Charles looks apprehensive during his first flying lesson in Sussex.

COLLEGE CAPERS: The lighter side of life at Cambridge — Charles and other cast members in a comedy sketch for a stage revue.

OUT ON THE MOORS: Diana takes it easy while others watch the sport.

To celebrate his twenty-fourth birthday, Charles dances a jig at Balmoral with his eight-year-old cousin, Lady Sarah Armstrong-Jones. His kilt is the Balmoral tartan.

DASHING DAREDEVIL PRINCE: Royal jockey Charles spurs on his horse in the Mad Hatters Race at Plumpton.
AND NOT-SO-DASHING: Four days of growth of beard on the royal face after Charles returned from a trek through the Himalayan mountains at the end of his tour of India.

DIANA SMILES THROUGH!: As rumours grew about her romance with Charles, Diana had photographers following her everywhere. She kept smiling, though she blushed when she realized the skirt she wore for pictures at the kindergarten was see-through!

'Uncle Dickie' – though Lord Mountbatten was his great-uncle he was more like a grandfather.

Tall and proud and handsome, Mountbatten had been a great British hero, a wartime leader and the last governor-general of India who, late in life, became a favourite television 'star' presenting documentary programmes.

In fact, he introduced a film about his own life story but gave strict instructions that it was to be shown only after his death. It was screened within hours of the explosion, and in it Mountbatten paid great tribute to Charles.

The tragedy happened as 'Uncle Dickie' and members of his family set sail one morning from a small harbour for a day's fishing. Irish terrorists had planted a bomb on board, and when it went off it killed not only Mountbatten but his grandson, fourteen-year-old Nicholas Knatchbull – who was also Charles's godson – and the Dowager Baroness Brabourne, who was eighty-two. On the same day, many miles away at Warrenpoint in Northern Ireland, sixteen paratroopers were killed by terrorist bombs. It was a terrible day in the long, violent history of Ireland's troubles.

Charles and his father, Prince Philip, went to Eastleigh Airport near Southampton when Lord Mountbatten's body was flown home. The funeral service at Westminster Abbey was followed by a private committal service at Romsey Abbey, close to Lord Mountbatten's lovely home at Broadlands.

Among the wreaths was one with the message: 'To my H.G.F. and G.U. from his loving and devoted H.G.S. and G.N.' De-coded, it meant: 'To my honorary grandfather and great-uncle, from his loving and devoted honorary grandson and great-nephew.'

Charles also attended the memorial service for the sixteen paratroopers who were killed, and read the Lesson. Later, in November, he made a surprise six-hour visit to Northern Ireland to see three of 'his' regiments – the Gordon Highlanders, the Prince of Wales's Company of the Welsh Guards, and the Parachute Regiment.

The following year, 1980, Charles went to India, a country much loved by his H.G.F., who had been in charge of the difficult task of arranging independence for India back in 1947. For many years until then, India had been part of the British Empire.

Charles travelled widely across the vast country. In Calcutta, he was visibly moved by the orphans he saw in a home run by Mother Theresa, who won the Nobel Peace Prize for her wonderful work amongst the poorest of the poor. He took particular interest in a tiny baby which had been found the day before in a dustbin.

In total contrast, there was trouble for a beautiful teenage actress, Padmini Kolhapure, who kissed Charles during his visit to a film studio in Bombay. Later, she appeared in court charged with 'denigrating Indian culture and womanhood by kissing in public.' In Indian films, kissing is banned!

After his tour, Charles travelled to the Himalayan mountain kingdom of Nepal for a week's holiday – including a three-day trek into the hills, guided by Pertemba Sherpa, who was a member of Chris Bonington's Everest expedition in 1975. Charles even found time to paint several watercolours, making full use of the very special light in the mountains. 'I can only do landscapes – very badly!' he said.

As a roving royal ambassador, Charles is at his brilliant best – relaxed, dignified, good-humoured. Advance parties plan the tour, checking on routes and security, making sure that everyone knows how to behave in the presence of the Prince of Wales. British diplomats give him a lot of information about the country he is visiting, and advise him on the subjects to steer clear of in speeches or in general conversation, for he must not in any way become involved in the politics of that country.

But, like other members of the royal family, he likes to get close to the people. Their walkabouts can cause real anxiety for the security men who protect them. In Canada during Jubilee Year Charles met members of the Blackfoot tribe of Indians, and put on the head-dress of the tribal chief. With Prince Andrew, who was then at school in Canada, he went to the Calgary Stampede dressed in a cowboy suit and leather boots.

In October of the same year, he flew back to North America for a whirlwind tour of twelve cities in the United States. At a glittering dinner for charity in Hollywood, he sat between Farah Fawcett, one of the TV stars of the detective series 'Charlie's Angels' and Angie Dickinson, from another top television series 'Policewoman'. And he commented: 'Two of the most beautiful cops I have ever seen.'

In fact not even Hollywood, the centre of the world's cinema industry, could have created a better man for the starring role of Prince of Wales than Charles Philip Arthur George.

He believes that, in the end, the job for which he has

been so rigorously trained is all about leadership. In an interview with *Radio Times* he said: 'I cannot relate it to anything else. I think it is trying to set an example, to help push people along, to be encouraging, to warn, advise, amuse . . . Everything to give people pleasure and a sense of purpose in life, a sense of satisfaction, a sense of feeling they have done something useful by congratulating them and generally being seen to show interest when it's deserved. It all, I hope and feel, goes towards trying to make as happy a society or country as possible.'

3
The Princess's Story

When the Princess of Wales drove through the snow in her Ford Escort to meet children at the local junior school near her new home at Tetbury in Gloucestershire, Kermit the Frog went too. Not the real puppet from the Muppets TV show, but a little mascot of him, fixed to her car.

Diana is a great fan of the Muppets, and does a pretty good impression of Kermit. Like her husband, she has a 'mad-cap' sense of humour – Charles loved a zany radio show many years ago called 'The Goons' and counts its stars, Sir Harry Secombe, Spike Milligan and Michael Bentine amongst his friends.

The Princess will find that sense of humour very useful in the years to come – being one of the most famous women in the world and a future Queen brings lots of pressures, and a good giggle now and then will help to ease the strain.

But with her background and her personality, she is well equipped for the job. If Charles didn't exactly marry 'the girl next door', he did the next best thing. Diana's first home was at Park House, on the Queen's estate at Sandringham. And she has royal blood in her veins – one of her far distant relatives was the seventeenth-century king, Charles the Second.

And long before she started going out with Prince Charles, there were modern-day connections between her family and the royals.

In fact, Diana is the only one of the four Spencer children who hasn't got a royal godparent. The Queen is a godparent to her younger brother, Charles, and the Queen Mother is a godparent to both her elder sisters, Sarah and Jane.

Diana's grandmother, Ruth Lady Fermoy, is a lady-in-waiting to the Queen Mother, and also a great friend. So was her other grandmother, the late Countess Spencer. And her father, Earl Spencer, was for some time an equerry – an official assistant – to the Queen.

So, for all her life, Diana has lived in the shadow of the royal family, and now she has become one of its brightest stars. She was born on 1 July 1961, and christened at Sandringham. Prince Andrew and Prince Edward were two of her favourite playmates: when they were staying at Sandringham they would nip over to Park House and use the Spencer's swimming pool.

Diana was too young to remember the first time she saw Prince Charles. He was twelve, and she was in nappies! But later she often stayed at Windsor Castle and Balmoral, where Charles organized treasure hunts to keep the younger children amused.

It was a happy, normal childhood for Diana Frances Spencer – marred when she was six years old by her parents' separation. Their wedding at Westminster Abbey in 1954 had been a great society occasion. But now her mother had left home – and a bitter divorce case followed.

Later, her mother married Peter Shand-Kydd and moved to north-west Scotland, where they run a sheep farm. It must have been a sad time for the Spencer children, but they got over it, and for Diana, school life was underway.

Her first lessons were with her governess, Gertrude Allen, who later said Diana was 'not particularly bright . . . but she did try!' And then – though no one could have guessed it at the time – Diana began to make history as the first Queen-to-be to go to an ordinary school.

When she was eight, she became a boarder at Riddlesworth Hall at Diss in Norfolk, about forty miles from her home. 'I remember her very well – she was a normal, ordinary little girl,' said Miss Elizabeth Ridsdale, who was headmistress there for thirty years until her retirement in 1976.

'She was always kind and cheerful, and she was especially good with the younger girls. If a new child was homesick and a bit miserable, you would notice Diana keeping an eye on her, comforting her. Even at that age, she showed great concern for others.'

Riddlesworth Hall has a reputation for being a friendly school with a secure, family-like atmosphere. Just the place for a young girl whose own family life was a little unsettled because of her parents' divorce. 'We like to think we helped her,' Miss Ridsdale told me.

Girls were allowed to bring their favourite cuddly toys and a few of their games from home. There was also a 'Pets Corner', where they kept their pet hamsters, rabbits and guinea pigs. But they had to look after them properly – if they didn't, the pets were sent home.

'Diana brought her guinea pig, Peanuts, and I think that in her last year she ended up in charge of Pets Corner,' said Miss Ridsdale. 'She was a dear little girl, and I like to think the school gave her confidence and a good start in life. She already had plenty of pluck.

'I was very pleased that she won a very special cup, the Helpfulness Cup. This was given by the teachers to any child who had been helpful in many ways without seeking praise or reward. The staff discussed spontaneous acts of kindness that they had spotted, and Diana was awarded the cup.'

Miss Ridsdale was adored by all the girls. They nicknamed her 'Riddy', and never thought twice about running to her if they had a problem. On the first night of every term, she went to every dormitory to say good night to the girls – and she allowed them to climb trees in the school's lovely grounds.

'At one of our first school council meetings, when staff and form captains talked about various matters, one of the girls asked if they could climb trees. My heart sank. I explained that if anyone got hurt, I would be to blame. "I know," said the girl. "If we write to our parents and ask them for permission to climb trees, and they say yes, it will be their responsibility." So that's what happened, and the parents were very good about it. I don't think we ever had any ghastly accidents!'

Did Diana go tree-climbing? 'She certainly did, and knowing her, I expect she got to the top,' smiled Miss Ridsdale. She remembers once driving towards the school, and seeing lots of red shapes in a small copse of beech trees. At first, she thought they were large birds, but when she got closer, she realized they were some of her tree-clambering pupils in their red blazers!

'Diana was always a lovely little girl, and now she is so beautiful,' said 'Riddy'. 'I hope that her four years at Riddlesworth Hall taught her the right kind of values in life, and to live with other people and respect them. Of course, no teacher expects one of their pupils to become a future queen! It was a great thrill for the school and for myself.'

To celebrate Diana's wedding day, Riddy was planning to hold a party with friends. Instead, she was invited to St Paul's Cathedral. 'It was the proudest day of my life,' she told me.

While she was at Riddlesworth Hall, dressed in the regulation uniform of white shirt, red jersey and grey divided skirt, Diana immersed herself in its happy life. She enjoyed English, and was good at games, especially swimming, which was well taught. She also loved riding, though later she lost her confidence after falling from a horse. Holidays were spent either with her father in Norfolk or her mother in Scotland.

Then when she was thirteen Diana moved to West Heath, at Sevenoaks in Kent, where she joined 130 other teenagers from well-to-do families in a large old house set in more than thirty acres of grounds.

To get accepted there, pupils have to pass the Common Entrance exams in subjects like general knowledge, geography, art, music, maths and French. Just as at her old school, Diana quickly became known for her kindness and cheerfulness, but in class she was only average.

A girl who was at West Heath with Diana told me: 'She was a typical, giggly, fun-to-know schoolgirl, and she used to be naughty during prep [homework]. She started in the first form, which is called Cedar. All the forms are named after trees – the top one is Oak.

'Girls in the younger forms sleep in rooms with between four and eight beds, and all the bedrooms are named after flowers such as Delphinium, White Rose, Snowdrop. The bedsteads are iron, with lumpy mattresses and the heating wasn't very efficient.' Older girls have their own small cubicle bedrooms.

While she was at West Heath, Diana was given an award for service which is only presented to outstanding pupils and the school's highest accolade. She seemed rather surprised when she won it, and also got prizes for ballet and tap. One school friend remembers her entertaining the others with a dancing display – rock 'n' roll, Charleston, ballet and jive.

Diana also became an excellent swimmer and a graceful diver – 'She made no splash,' said one schoolmate, enviously.

Other girls remember a pillow fight which ended abruptly when Diana's pillow went flying out of the window and crashed down on to the headmistress's shrubbery! The head, Miss Ruth Rudge, is said to be kind but firm – and her thoughts about the pillow fight aren't on record! But she is tall, distinguished-looking and much liked.

In Diana's last year, she became a prefect and, among other things, that entitled her to wear trousers in class!

This was a typical day at West Heath while its most famous old girl was a pupil there:

7.30. Rising bell. Matron came round at twenty to eight to check that everyone was out of bed.

8.00. Breakfast bell. If you were late for breakfast you had to report, and then arrive at five minutes to eight for a week! Breakfast was cereal, scrambled eggs or fried bread and baked beans, with bread and margarine. Only on Sundays was there butter. After breakfast, the girls went upstairs to make their beds and tidy their rooms.

9.00. Bell for prayers, which lasted about ten minutes. First lessons were at *9.20*, after a short talk with the form-mistress. Three lessons of thirty-five minutes each, going from class to class, then break – two plain digestive biscuits and milk.

Afterwards, three more lessons before lunch.

1.20. Lunch bell. A member of staff sat at each table, and a typical meal would be 'meat, two veg. and stodge'.

2.00 bell. Juniors to rest, seniors to play games three days a week.

3.00. Juniors games, seniors free.

4.00 Tea. Bread and marge, usually with cakes on Tuesdays, Thursdays and at weekends.

4.20. Four more lessons, or prep. Older girls took younger ones for prep.

7.05. Quarter of an hour of 'free time' until supper at *7.20*. Then more free time after supper, although no one was allowed to go up to their bedrooms. Some might go to the music room or the gym, or play tennis in summer.

8.25. Juniors to bed, lights out at *9.00*.

Older girls stay up later, but those in the final year had to have their lights out by *10.30*.

Every girl had three baths a week, and were given a set time for them. Maybe 6.35 on Tuesdays, Thursdays and Saturdays, or 7.45 on Mondays, Wednesdays and Fridays.

In 1975, while Diana was still at West Heath, her grandfather died. Her father became the eighth Earl Spencer and moved to Althorp, the family seat in Northamptonshire. Althorp is a beautiful stately home, built three centuries ago in the time of King Charles the Second.

There's been a Spencer family home at Althorp for even longer. The land was bought in 1508 by John Spencer, a local dignitary who was later knighted by King Henry the Eighth. Althorp is set in 1500 acres of beautiful English countryside, and the Spencers have been farmers for centuries.

They were also patrons of the arts, and the house has many fine paintings by artists like Gainsborough, Van Dyck and Rubens. In the days before photography, wealthy families like the Spencers had their portraits painted – and the house is full of paintings of Diana's forebears, looking down from the walls in the ornately decorated frames.

One of them, Jack, third Earl Spencer, preferred farming to fine art, and he made sure that pictures of his prize shorthorn cattle hung amongst the family portraits! Jack was also a politician and became Chancellor of the Exchequer.

The Spencer family tree is quite remarkable, and it branches off in all kinds of unexpected directions. *Burke's Peerage*, that well-known reference book about the aristocracy, says that among Diana's distant relations were film stars Rudolph Valentino, the great heart-throb of silent movies, and Humphrey Bogart, who was a seventh cousin. And she's also related to Prince Charles in other ways – by connections going back to King Henry the Eighth they are sixteenth cousins, once removed! And through another royal connection, they are seventh cousins, once removed!

For many generations, the Spencers have cared for and cherished Althorp, none more so than the seventh Earl, Diana's grandfather. I read that he was a close friend of Queen Mary and, like her, was very keen on embroidery. Neither of them could have imagined that one day their families would weave together like the tapestries they loved – with the marriage of Queen Mary's great-grandson to the Earl's grand-daughter!

After his death, Althorp passed to Diana's father who inherited not only a beautiful home, but also the headache of running such a massive place with all its modern-day costs. A year later Earl Spencer married again, to an outspoken, colourful lady called Raine, the former Countess of Dartmouth. So the Spencer children now had a step-mother, and a very well-known step-mother, for Raine is the daughter of Barbara Cartland, author of hundreds of romantic novels and a frequent guest on television chat shows.

Raine brought a new regime to Althorp, and at first some of the staff didn't take too kindly to her ways. But in 1978, she showed her love for her husband in a quite outstanding way. The Earl collapsed with a massive brain hemorrhage, and he would almost certainly have died had it not been for Raine's determination that he would get better.

She arranged a private ambulance for him, switched him from hospital to hospital and specialist to specialist, searching for the best treatment. She managed to get hold of a 'miracle' drug which wasn't available in this country, but which had been used successfully on the continent. She tracked down supplies of it which were being tested in Britain and persuaded doctors to use it on the Earl.

All the time, she never left his side and even played him his favourite piece of music from 'Madame Butterfly'. Gradually, the Earl became conscious again and slowly got better, though he still has slight problems with his speech.

For Diana then came the big question – what to do when she left West Heath? Diana's next move, as it turned out, was a wrong one. She said good-bye to West Heath, taking a last look at the old building where she'd spent so many happy days, and headed for Switzerland. She enrolled at a finishing school called the Institut Alpin Videmanette where she studied domestic science, dressmaking, cooking and French, and also went skiing. But she only stayed there for six weeks – she was too home-sick.

Throughout her young life, Diana had always loved children, so it wasn't surprising that she should look for a job that involved looking after them. For a year, she helped care for a little boy called Patrick whose American parents were living in London – later, they were invited to the wedding.

She also worked at the Young England kindergarten in London's Pimlico, run by Kay King and Vicky Wilson. Diana went there three afternoons a week at first, as an assistant helping to look after the youngest ones. The school has about seventy children, aged from two and a half to five, and after a term or so, Diana liked the work so much she went there for three full days a week.

'She was very good at her job, and everyone loved her,' Mrs King told me. 'She was with us for about two years, and she helped with all kinds of activities – painting, music, dancing, singing, puzzles – and clearing up the mess!'

Mrs King knew Diana through their families. When the press were besieging the nursery, it was a difficult time for the staff. 'But life at the kindergarten went on totally unchanged,' Mrs King told me. 'Amazingly, Diana managed to shut away all the fuss as soon as she walked through the door.'

Another colleague there spoke of Diana's friendly and sensible nature, adding, 'She was always very co-operative and always busy.'

Her father bought her a flat in Coleherne Court – experts say it was worth £100,000 – and she moved in with three friends: Carolyn Pride, who'd also been to West Heath and who was studying singing and music; Anne Bolton, secretary to an estate agent – she and Diana met on a skiing holiday; and Virginia Pitman, a Cordon Bleu cook.

Though she was what used to be called 'a flower of the English aristocracy', she didn't launch herself full-swing into the London social scene. She liked going to the cinema, and popping into pubs with friends – though she doesn't really like alcohol. She enjoyed shopping at stores like Harrods and Liberty's, and browsing along Bond Street.

Her flatmates said she was a lot of fun, and called her a 'homemaker'. She did have one bad habit – biting her fingernails! But everyone who knows her, or who knew her, repeats the same message when asked what Diana is really like – 'kind, cheerful and sweet'.

On the day her engagement was announced, her father described her as 'a perfect physical specimen'. He added: 'She never breaks down – she has great courage and resilience.'

Diana loves the outdoor life, going salmon fishing and skiing. She doesn't smoke – like Prince Charles she detests the habit. Among her 'likes' are chocolate, and scrambled eggs. She enjoys music, and plays the piano, and is an avid reader. And before she got her red Mini Metro, she used to go by bike round London.

Suddenly, that free-and-easy lifestyle changed. As the Princess of Wales she can't go biking round London, or pop into a pub, or go to the cinema, or look round the shops for bargains.

She was still a teenager when the Prince proposed marriage, and just a few months before that special day no one had ever heard of her except her family and friends. Now, her face is known all over the world. But she's brought something new and fresh to the royal family, and everyone hopes that it won't get stifled by all the formality of life in the royal court.

She only had three years from leaving school to becoming a Princess, but she packed a lot into them. And if and when Charles becomes King, his Queen will be the first one ever to have worked for a living!

4
Previous Princesses

In Britain's history, there have only been nine Princesses of Wales. The first was Joan, Countess of Kent, who married the Black Prince – son of Edward III – in 1361.

The only Princess of Wales in her own right – not getting the title by marrying the Prince – was Mary Tudor. She was made Princess of Wales by her father, King Henry the Eighth.

Our present Prince and Princess married because they fell in love, but that hasn't always been the case. More than 200 years ago when royal marriages were 'arranged', the Prince who later became King George the Fourth said after his first meeting with his bride-to-be, Princess Caroline of Brunswick-Wolfenbuttel: 'I am not well, pray get me a glass of brandy!'

A previous Lady Diana Spencer once turned down a Prince of Wales. She was born in 1708 and was the daughter of Charles Spencer, Earl of Sunderland and Lady Anne Churchill. Her grandmother, the Duchess of Marlborough, wanted to arrange a match between Diana and Frederick Louis, son of George the Second. But that particular Prince of Wales didn't appeal at all to that Lady Diana.

The present Diana became the first English fiancée

of an heir to the throne for 300 years, and their wedding was the first of an English bride to a future King of England since 1659, when Charles the First's son, James, married Anne Hyde.

The wedding was also the first by a Prince of Wales since 1863, when Edward, later King Edward III, married Alexandra.

Name

Some critics have been worrying about the name Diana – they say that Queen Diana doesn't seem very regal. I think it sounds rather beautiful compared to some of the names our queens have had since the Norman Conquest. Here they all are:

ADELAIDE
ALEXANDRA
ANNE
BERENGARIA
CAROLINE
CHARLOTTE
ELEANOR
ELIZABETH
HENRIETTA
ISABEL
ISABELLA
JANE
JOAN
KATHERINE
KATHARINE
MARGARET
MARY

MATILDA
PHILIPPA
SOPHIA
VICTORIA

5
Run-up to the Wedding

As soon as the engagement was announced, just about the whole of Britain caught Royal Wedding fever. Lots of questions had still to be answered. Would the wedding be at Westminster Abbey or St Paul's Cathedral? What date would it be? How many bridesmaids, and who would they be? Who would make the dress? Where would Charles and Diana go for their honeymoon? Long before we knew all those answers, newspapers and television shows were making guesses.

Experts on anything to do with royalty were called upon to give their predictions. Some turned out to be correct, others were way off mark. The writers who picked St Paul's for the wedding got it right – the great event would be held there on Wednesday, 29 July. St Paul's was chosen because it can hold more people, and the way sound swells through the massively impressive building made it ideal for the musical wedding that was being planned.

There were to be five bridesmaids – the eldest seventeen-year-old Lady Sarah Armstrong-Jones, the daughter of Princess Margaret. The others would be India Hicks, fourteen, Sarah Jane Gaselee, ten, Catherine Cameron, six, and five-year-old Clementine Hambro, a pupil at the Young England kindergarten where Lady Diana worked before her engagement. There would also be two pages – Lord Nicholas Windsor, the eleven-year-old son of the Duke and Duchess of Kent, and eight-year-old Edward Van Cutsem.

The honour of making the bride's dress went to a young husband-and-wife team of designers, David and Elizabeth Emmanuel. They were also asked to make the bridesmaids' dresses. The design of Lady Diana's was kept top secret until the moment she appeared in the glass coach on her way to St Paul's.

All that the Emmanuels would say beforehand was that it would transform her into a 'fairytale princess'. They added: 'She is young, fresh and lovely and the dress should reflect all that.'

Diana's wedding ring was to be made from a nugget of Welsh gold from the Clogau St David's mine in North Wales. The nugget was given to the royal family at the turn of the century, and it had already provided wedding rings for the Queen Mother, the Queen, Princess Margaret and Princess Anne. And the last of the gold left from that nugget was fashioned for Diana by the royal jewellers, Collingwood.

The setting for the honeymoon was a guessing game, and the nearest anyone got was that the royal yacht *Britannia* would take the couple cruising in the Mediterranean.

In fact, I got a better clue than most. The year before, I had filmed a television series called 'Breakthrough' about great engineers, and one of the programmes was on the life of Ferdinand de Lesseps, who built the Suez Canal. Later, a letter arrived from the *Britannia* asking if it would be possible to have a copy of the script to show the crew as the ship would be sailing in that area in the future. As it turned out, the *Britannia* went down the Suez Canal with the honeymoon couple on board!

But that was months ahead, and as the excitement began to build there was a new fashion trend, the 'Lady Di Look'. The prize in one competition was an identical suit to the one she wore on the day the engagement was announced, and there were nation-wide contests to find Lady Di look-alikes.

Sales boomed of the lipstick, eyeliner and other make-up which would give the Diana look. Her hair-style was copied by millions of teenage girls across the world, so much so that while Prince Charles was on a visit to New Zealand he came face to face with a group of Diana look-alikes on one of his walkabouts. At first, he seemed rather annoyed thinking, no doubt, it was a publicity stunt, but it was passed off as just a bit of fun.

Lady Diana was *the* fashion setter. Her first public appearance with the Prince after their engagement was a recital in Goldsmith's Hall to raise money for the Royal Opera House. She wore a black taffeta dress, designed by the Emmanuels, and the crowds gasped when they saw it – not only was it stunning, but it was low-cut and she had to be very careful as she got out of the car!

Princess Grace of Monaco was also at the function, and people noted that Diana had to curtsey to her. After the wedding, they would greet each other as equals.

On 27 March, the Queen gave her formal consent to the marriage – something which has to happen under the Royal Marriages Act. Oliver Everett was appointed as Lady Diana's secretary – his job was to look after the formalities on her behalf at the meetings which were held to plan the wedding.

Her Mini Metro was replaced by a new Ford Escort Ghia, and she also travelled in Charles's Ford Granada estate or a Royal Mews Rolls-Royce.

She watched Charles race at Sandown, where he fell off his horse Good Prospect, and she was also to see him hunting as the head of the Cheshire Hunt during a weekend at Cholmondeley Castle.

Among their official visits was one to the little town of Tetbury in Gloucestershire, just down the road from the lovely country house which would be their home after the wedding.

Diana went on her own to the tennis tournament at Wimbledon, where she watched the singles finals. After Chris Evert won the ladies' championship, she and her husband John Lloyd had tea with Diana, who apparently confessed that she was so nervous about the wedding that she didn't know how she was going to cope.

Only a few days before the big event, she left a polo match in tears and wasn't able to present the prize. All the attention and all the pressure had just become too much. In the months before the wedding, she lost nearly a stone in weight, probably through nerves.

Throughout the land, great festivities were being planned for 29 July – street parties, bonfires, banquets in hotels. The tourist trade boomed as many thousands of foreign visitors arrived in Britain to join in the celebrations. The wedding day was declared a national holiday, and that led to some grumbles from industry. Why couldn't a Friday have been chosen? Bosses and trade union leaders said the day off would cost millions of pounds in lost production, and it would have been much cheaper for firms to close down their factories on a Thursday for a long weekend rather than turn things off on a Tuesday and start up again on Thursday.

But one branch of industry wasn't complaining – the firms making souvenirs. From commemorative mugs to beautiful bone china loving cups at £250 each, from T-shirts to hand-painted vases costing £2140, the production lines were buzzing. To make sure everything was in good taste, a Royal Wedding Souvenir Selection Panel was set up, headed by Lord Snowdon.

At dawn on 26 July, there was a rehearsal of the procession to St Paul's, using the horse-drawn carriages. The next day, much to the delight of unsuspecting sightseers, was a rehearsal of the wedding itself at the cathedral. Charles nearly tripped up the stairs, and Diana practised with a length of mock veil and measured the steps she would need to take.

On the same day more than 5000 London children took part in the longest street party ever held. The 861 bunting-strewn tables stretched for one and a quarter miles along London's Oxford Street, and was paid for by the owners of the street's shops. The young guests got through ten tons of food and drink and were given another ten tons of wedding souvenirs and gifts.

Entertaining them were fire-eaters, stilt-walkers, tap dancers, pop bands, pipe bands, pearly kings and conjurors. The party began with the arrival of 'Prince

Charles and Lady Diana' in an open carriage. In fact they were Jane and Matthew Gale, aged eleven and nine, and Jane admitted that it was 'a little frightening' facing all the cameras.

The party cost £10,000, got into the record books, and for everyone who took part it was a smashing start to Royal Wedding Week.

By this time, the first of the crowds were camping along the route in sleeping bags, determined to get the best views of the processions – and, on the eve of the wedding, the great firework display in Hyde Park . . . the one that Diana missed because she was having an 'early night'. Anyway, tradition has it that it's unlucky for a bride and groom to meet on the night before their wedding.

The royal family, including Charles, joined half a million well-wishers in the park for the magnificent display, costing £1000 a minute and based round a giant fireworks palace nearly 100 metres long and ten metres high, made from scaffolding and canvas. At seven minutes past ten – a few minutes late – Charles started the celebrations by lighting a fuse with a flaming torch. That in turn lit a beacon, and its flame was spotted by look-outs high up in the Telecom Tower. They flashed the news to Windsor, where the second beacon was to be lit, and by eleven o'clock more than a hundred beacons all around the British Isles were aflame. At Althorp, Lady Diana's home in Northamptonshire, the beacon was lit by her brother, Viscount Althorp.

Back in Hyde Park, an amazing display of fireworks shattered the darkness with a rainbow of exploding colours. The finale was a huge Catherine wheel, nearly eleven metres wide, bearing the letters C and D.

When the fun was over, Charles and the rest of the royal family returned to Buckingham Palace. The crowds, far bigger than expected, spilled out into roads and dozens of people were slightly hurt in the crush to get through the gates.

There were traffic jams till the early hours as thousands of people headed for home and a few hours' sleep before watching the wedding on television. Others didn't bother to go home – they strolled down to the route and rested on pavements and in parks until the great day dawned.

6

In Front of the Cameras

On the night before her wedding, Lady Diana had a special word of thanks to all the children who had sent gifts. 'They have obviously spent hours of work on paintings, pictures, cards and things like that. And the things they've baked at home – it's wonderful.'

One of the cakes 'had so many Smarties you could hardly see what it is'. And she revealed that she had been given a special present – a collage – by the children she helped to look after at the Young England kindergarten.

The pattern showed the giant firework display that was being planned in St James's Park that night – 'the one I'm not going to,' smiled Lady Diana. 'I'm going to be tucked up in bed, I think – early night!'

She said she collected the collage when she went to end of term party at the kindergarten 'where I ended up being battered and bruised, I had so many children crawling on top of me. But they presented me with that, and a glass representing Young England. It was lovely, really nice.'

Lady Diana was talking during a television interview that she and Prince Charles had with Angela Rippon and Andrew Gardner in the lovely summer house of Buckingham Palace. The couple looked relaxed and happy, with Lady Diana betraying just a sign of nerves in the way she fiddled with her earring.

As it's one of the few interviews they have given together, it's worth looking back on some of the things they said on the eve of the great day.

They were obviously thrilled by the public reaction to their engagement and wedding. Said Lady Diana: 'It's been a tremendous boost – just a mass of smiling faces. It's wonderful.'

Prince Charles added: 'The most overwhelming and touching reactions. I, of course, went to New Zealand and Australia and Venezuela, and then America on the way back. This was in April and May. And the people were amazingly friendly and enthusiastic. And since then, all the times I've been round different parts of the country here, the reaction has been literally fantastic. I've never seen so many people around and such friendliness and overwhelming sort of generosity.'

Andrew Gardner mentioned the thousands of people who were joining in the festivities in a practical way, organizing street parties and collecting for charities. Had Prince Charles become involved in that?

'Not so personally involved, but I've tried to make sure I'm informed of what's going on,' replied the Prince. 'The difficulty is there is so much coming in in terms of mail and presents that it's hard to keep up, especially when you try to dash about the country as well.

'Already this week alone I hear there have been

25,000 letters and it's averaged 15,000 letters for the last four weeks. I think roughly since we got engaged there have been about 100,000 letters. I wanted to be able to say how really grateful we are for such incredible kindness. I can't get over it. And I think there have been something like 3000 . . . over 3000 presents.'

The couple went on to talk about the wedding service at St Paul's. They both love the cathedral, and Lady Diana said it would take about three and a half minutes to walk up the aisle. That's one of the reasons why they had picked stirring music. Explained Prince Charles: 'If you have something rather quiet you start hearing your ankles cricking.'

He said he'd always longed for a musical wedding, and had a lot of fun organizing the music. 'I can't wait for the whole thing,' he said. 'I want everybody to come out having had a marvellous musical and emotional experience.'

Lady Diana said she had chosen one hymn, 'I Vow To Thee My Country', which had always been her favourite since schooldays.

Then Angela Rippon spoke about the wedding vows, saying that when any couple makes such vows it is the most solemn, most precious and very personal moment. And she wondered: 'Is it going to be the same for you, even though you know the eyes of the world are watching you?'

Prince Charles replied: 'I hope so, yes. I mean, I don't know about Diana, but I'm more used to it I think, knowing for years that there are cameras poking at you and recording every twitch you make.

'So you can get used to it to a certain extent and on those occasions you accept that that's part of it. I think that if you don't try to work out in your own mind some kind of method for existing and surviving this kind of thing, you would go mad. And so, in the end, you get used to it.'

Then, turning to his bride-to-be, he asked: 'Do you find after the last six months you're beginning to get used to it?'

'Just,' she said, adding that Prince Charles had been giving her a great deal of help. He'd been a tower of strength.

'Gracious!' said the Prince.

'I had to say that,' said Diana with a smile, ''cos you're sitting there.'

Andrew Gardner then asked Lady Diana how she saw her role developing as the Princess of Wales. She replied: 'I very much look forward to going to Wales and meeting everybody, but my life will be a great challenge.'

She said that children were her particular interest, but her interests would broaden as the years went on. 'As I'm twenty, I've got a good start,' she said.

The next question was about public engagements – would they be carrying them out separately or together?

'Well, I think quite a lot will be joint, obviously, and certainly to begin with,' said Prince Charles. 'And I think obviously when we go abroad they'll be joint. But I think that as Diana begins to do various things or gets involved in the children's things that very often you get many more invitations, you meet more people, you suddenly find areas or things that you think: "My goodness I must . . . I'd like to do something about improving things here, or encouraging there."

'And after a bit you develop your own sphere. This is what I found because I was about twenty when I launched, or was launched, on to the scene. But I think to start with we will do quite a lot together.'

Lady Diana said she was looking forward very much to making a home at Highgrove and 'being a good wife'. She said she'd taken a cookery course, but hadn't allowed Prince Charles to sample any of her cooking – yet.

Towards the end of the interview, Prince Charles returned to the problems of being members of the royal family, while trying to have an ordinary family life.

He said: 'It's the most difficult thing, trying to work out how you can have a family life as well as all the public demands that there are. I lead a sort of idiotic existence, trying to get involved in too many things and dashing about.

'And this is going to be my problem, trying to sort of control myself and work out something so that we can have a proper family life.

'It isn't easy. There's so much to be done, you know.'

7
The Big Day

At six o'clock in the morning on 29 July 1981, I stood on the embankment of the river Thames and watched a great red ball of sun rising through the early mist beyond St Paul's Cathedral. It was the start of a beautiful summer's day – and of a wedding day filled with as much warmth as the sun that shone down on it.

I'd already been awake for three hours, filming reports for the special breakfast-time television programme on BBC 1. As dawn broke, streets along and around the route were thronged with people, and as I strolled along The Mall sleepy heads were stirring, sleeping bags were being packed away, and happy sing-songs filled the air which, at that hour, is normally left to the birds.

Flags and banners were already waving, and there were great cheers for the street-cleaners as they made sure that, for once, the roads were free of litter. An elderly lady from South Wales told me: 'We've had a lovely night. Everybody's been so friendly and we're not a bit tired. I wouldn't have missed it for anything.' And, turning to her friend from the same Welsh valley, she added: 'After all, it's our prince who's getting married today.'

A little further along The Mall I came across a group of university students wearing evening dress. They'd spent the night on the pavement in style – having a six-course dinner served to them, complete with wines, napkins and tablecloth. 'We decided to eat out,' grinned one of them.

The tremendous feeling of good-humour in that early morning crowd was to grow even stronger as the day continued, and I was struck by the large number of young people gathering along the route. Cub packs arrived in coaches, punks had dyed their hair red, white and blue; young mums and dads held their toddlers above their heads so they could see the view. Critics who say that royalty is going out of fashion amongst the young should have been down on The Mall that morning.

Mingling amongst everyone, chatting and joking and getting to know their little bit of the crowd along the two-mile route, were the police. Thousands of blue uniforms belonging to the only people along the route who wouldn't see much of the procession, because they had to keep their eyes fixed on the crowds. Security for the royal family and all the distinguished guests from abroad, many of them royal, was the daunting task of the police.

A terrorist group or a crank with a gun could turn this happy day into one of great tragedy, and the police were even more on their guard after the incident at the Trooping of the Colour ceremony earlier in the year when a teenager fired blanks towards the Queen. And the president of the United States, Ronald Reagan, was not attending the wedding – he was still recovering from an attempt on his life. So, as the 4000 police men and women made friends with the crowds, they were also on the look-out for anything suspicious.

Police marksmen were in position at vantage points, teams of detectives were on the alert behind the crowds, a police helicopter hovered over the route sending back television pictures to Scotland Yard, and two policemen dressed as footmen travelled in the procession – one on the Queen's coach, the other on Prince Charles's. They carried guns and two-way radios under their ceremonial clothes. Fortunately, this day of happiness and romance passed without a single threat to spoil it.

By eight o'clock, the crowds in The Mall and Trafalgar Square were so thick it was almost impossible to move, and those at the back were buying red, white and blue periscopes to see over the heads of those in front. I spotted one man with no such problems – he was on seven-foot stilts! But the best views were from windows looking down on to the route – and some of those windows had been hired out for the day at spectacular sums.

I was lucky because I had a grandstand view from Canada Gate, just opposite Buckingham Palace. From here, television crews from many countries were setting the scene for their viewers. American networks were presenting their breakfast shows live from Canada Gate, and it's reckoned that one in every ten people on earth heard the actual service, and seven hundred million watched it on television. Never before had so many 'guests' been 'invited' to a wedding!

The million or so people who were lining the route didn't miss out on the service – if they didn't have transistor radios or portable televisions, they could listen to it on the sixty loudspeakers strung out above them.

While the singing and the expectation was building up in the streets, Lady Diana was preparing herself in Clarence House. Hairdresser Kevin Shanley arrived in jeans to do her hair, and top make-up artist Barbara Daly worked on her lovely face. On went the shoes, handmade by Clive Shilton, and the dress that everyone was waiting to see. Amazingly, it *had* remained a secret, and although David and Elizabeth Emmanuel said they had other dresses ready if the details had leaked out, they later admitted they'd only been working on the one.

On the day before, an American newspaper called *Women's Wear Daily* tried to scoop the world by revealing what the dress would be like – but they got it wrong, because they said it would be 'entirely free of ornaments and surface decoration'.

In fact, the dress was a fairytale creation made of cream silk taffeta with an eighteen-carat gold horseshoe sewn into it for luck. The 'something old' was Carrickmacross lace, given to the Royal School of Needlework by Queen Mary, and used for the bodice. 'Something new' was the dress itself. 'Something borrowed' was the diamond tiara from the Spencer family collection and a pair of diamond drop earrings from Lady Diana's mother. 'Something blue' was a bow sewn into the waistband.

The Emmanuels were at Clarence House to help, and then dashed to the cathedral to smoothe out any last-minute wrinkles. Such was the interest in the dress that before the day was out, some shops had already run up copies and had them on display in their windows!

Outside the Palace, the crowds sang 'God Save the Queen' as the coach carrying Her Majesty left for the cathedral, and there was another great roar as the second coach came through the gates, with Queen Elizabeth the Queen Mother and Prince Edward.

The 2500 official guests were already taking their places as the bridegroom left the Palace with his brother and 'supporter', Prince Andrew, in the 1902 State Landau – a light maroon-coloured coach with lots of gold leaf, pulled by three light-grey geldings, Rio, Santiago, Sydney and Cardiff.

A few minutes later, Lady Diana and her father, Earl Spencer, left Clarence House in the Glass Coach – chosen because it has large windows so that everyone could see her. All along the route were flowers in pink, mauve and silver to contrast with the red of the uniforms, and a thousand flags fluttered from lamp-posts and flagpoles.

As the Glass Coach drove along the Strand, hundreds of pigeons were released from upper windows – they had a real 'bird's eye view' of all the splendour and excitement going on down below!

As Diana stepped from the coach outside St Paul's, the world got its first good look at *the* dress, with its magnificent train, twenty-five feet long, and its veil hand-embroidered with 10,000 tiny mother-of-pearl sequins. She asked some of the people nearby: 'Has he got here yet?' – and who else could that be but Prince Charles!

Of course, he was there – together with relatives and friends, colleagues and acquaintances, foreign dignitaries and important guests from Britain and the Commonwealth. Right in the front row sat Diana's flatmates. Mrs Nancy Reagan, wife of the American president, was a few rows back. There'd been concern that the Queen Mother might not be there, because she had recently hurt her leg. But she told the Dean: 'I would not have missed this for anything.'

As Diana waited with her father for the music to begin, lip-readers were hard at work. The Earl was a little unsteady on his feet after a serious illness, and apparently Diana said: 'Do you want to hold my arm as well for a moment?' (The Earl was holding the arm of an usher.)

He replied, say the lip-readers: 'I am all right. Really I am . . . walk now, shall we? Here we go. Go slowly.' And for three and a half minutes they walked up the aisle, to the marvellous sound of Jeremiah Clark's 'Trumpet Voluntary'. It heralded a service filled with joyful music.

The Archbishop of Canterbury, Dr Robert Runcie, performed the ceremony of marriage, assisted by clergymen of many denominations including the Roman Catholic Archbishop of Westminster, Cardinal Hume. At the moment the Cardinal was about to take part, independent television lost its picture from inside the cathedral for two minutes because of a power failure – but the BBC stepped in to help, and lent their pictures to ITV till things got back to normal.

When the time came to exchange their vows, Diana showed a charming trace of nervousness by getting the Prince's names mixed up. She was asked by Dr Runcie to take Charles Philip Arthur George as her wedded husband. Instead, she replied, 'I, Diana Frances, take thee, Philip Charles Arthur George,' and the Prince gave a little smile.

But the score was even when the Prince himself slipped up, forgetting the word 'worldly' from his pledge to share all his goods with his wife. Some people think he may even have done this on purpose, to make Diana feel better. Only they will know!

Dr Runcie, in his address, saw the 'fairytale' wedding not as the end of a romance but 'the place where the adventure really begins'. And as soon as the crowds outside heard the vows, great cheers went off, champagne corks popped, and round the gates of Buckingham Palace, the chant of 'Lady Di' quickly switched to 'Princess Di'.

And the lip-readers were still busy. According to them, this is what the couple said to each other at one stage of the ceremony:

Diana: Well, I'm glad that bit's over!

Charles: Yes. It's a marvellous sensation, isn't it? Look, there are our friends over there. Isn't it lovely!

Diana: Oh, everything is lovely.

Charles: Are you enjoying it? What do you make of your big day?

Diana replied with a radiant smile.

Though the television cameras had seen every moment of the ceremony, the couple signed the register in privacy. The New Zealand opera star Kiri Te Kanawa sang with stirring voice to the congregation and the world while Charles wrote in the register, Charles P, and Diana wrote, Diana Spencer.

Then, as husband and wife and Prince and Princess

of Wales, they walked down the aisle to the music of Elgar's 'Pomp and Circumstance'. At the cathedral door, there was an explosion of cheering, which never stopped or diminished for one second during their drive together to Buckingham Palace in the open state landau. The Princess's veil was swept back, so that everyone could see her face as the coach passed the forests of people, periscopes and waving plastic flags. Rice and petals were thrown at the couple from all directions. One little boy amongst the throng in The Mall told me excitedly that he'd seen Charles kiss Diana's hand.

Once the royal family was all safely back inside the Palace, the barriers holding back the crowd from the road outside came down, and a vast sea of people swept towards the gates, flooding The Mall from end to end. With one voice, they called for something which is a very special tradition to most Britons – the appearance of the royal family on the balcony.

At ten minutes past one the family and wedding party emerged through the tall french windows. Charles and Diana smiled and waved, and the crowd cheered madly.

After the first two appearances, the crowd started to chant 'We want the Queen' – and the monarch answered their call, elegant and smiling.

Then the chant changed to 'We want the Queen Mum', and she too stepped forward, remembering no doubt the time when she stood on that same balcony after her wedding nearly sixty years before.

Three times they disappeared behind the windows, and three times they reappeared to the delight of the half-million people below. The third time the couple appeared, Prince Andrew encouraged his elder brother, who then briefly kissed his bride. The crowd went wild. It was the first time members of the royal family had kissed in public.

After the final appearance, 120 guests consisting of members of the families and close friends sat down to the wedding breakfast in the ball-supper room of the Palace. Outside the crowd tucked in to sandwiches and hamburgers and waited for Charles and Diana to leave for their honeymoon.

The main dish at the breakfast was created in honour of the new Princess – Supreme de Volaille Princess de Galle, chicken breasts stuffed with lamb mousse served with a creamy mint sauce. Guests sat at tables of twelve, laid with white cloths and gold plate, and decorated with orchids. They ended their meal with strawberries and cream, and although many wedding cakes were on display, pride of place went to the one made by the Royal Naval Cookery School. Prince Charles cut it, using his dress sword. The toast to the happy couple was jointly proposed by Prince Andrew and Prince Edward.

The official wedding photographs were taken by top photographer Patrick Lichfield. Because it was such a big family group, he'd worked out in advance where everyone would stand and made marks on the carpet. When Diana showed signs of flagging, Charles stood behind Lord Lichfield and made faces at her, and among all the formal pictures, there's a wonderfully informal one – Prince Charles had just cracked a joke, and bridesmaids, pages and supporters collapsed in a fit of giggles.

Meanwhile, many of the guests at St Paul's were

making their way home. One who couldn't go back straightaway was the president of the tiny African country of the Gambia, Sir Dawda Jawara. He was deposed while the ceremony was going on, when some army officers took over his country. But a short while later, they were overthrown and Sir Dawda returned as president.

Other guests had included 170 staff from the royal homes at Sandringham, Windsor and Balmoral, and the lady who 'charred' for Prince Charles during his days at Cambridge University, sixty-one-year-old Mrs Flo Moore.

Also there had been Patrick and Mary Robertson, parents of two-year-old Patrick whom the Princess had helped look after for a year. They're an American couple, and Mrs Robertson had once been upset when Diana failed to turn up for work. All was forgiven, though, when she explained that she was being presented to the Queen!

An important guest who turned down an invitation was King Juan Carlos of Spain, who is a close personal friend of the royal family. His refusal was a political one: at the start of the honeymoon, the Prince and Princess were joining the royal yacht *Britannia* at Gibraltar – the tiny country run by Britain on the southern tip of Spain. For years, Spain has claimed that Gibraltar belongs to her – and the news that Charles and Diana were going there was taken as something of a diplomatic insult by the Spanish.

The honeymoon began in the middle of the afternoon, when the Prince and Princess left Buckingham Palace in the open carriage for Waterloo Station. Once again, the crowds cheered all the way, and laughed at a little touch which showed that this was an ordinary family occasion as well as a great royal event. Fixed to the carriage were blue and silver heart-shaped balloons bearing the Prince of Wales's crest. They'd been put there by Prince Andrew and Prince Edward, who were also responsible for scrawling a 'Just Married' sign on the back of the coach.

At the station, the royal couple boarded a private train for the one-hour journey to Romsey in Hampshire. From there, it was a short car drive to Broadlands, once the home of Prince Charles's beloved great uncle, Lord Mountbatten, who had been murdered by Irish terrorists.

There, a candlelit dinner for just the two of them was waiting. It had been a great day of national happiness, celebrated in a great cathedral, at a great palace, and by a mass of people in a great city. They'd been joined by millions round their television sets, and the toast to the happy couple had been raised at hundreds of street parties and thousands of private ones.

In London, the massive police operation was over – and there'd only been a handful of arrests. Even the horses had been well behaved, apart from one which ran off in Trafalgar Square. As the state coaches were locked away, 4000 other coaches – the diesel ones that most of us travel in – began taking people back home from London to every part of the country.

At 4.40 p.m., when live coverage of the honeymoon departure came to an end, the people of Britain did what they always do at the end of a big event – they made a cup of tea! So many kettles were switched on that demand for electricity jumped by 1800 megawatts

– that's like 180 extra towns each with 10,000 people suddenly plugging into the electricity system.

On the streets, nearly 209 tons of rubbish was cleared from the route and dumped on to tips in Essex. And of course, there were those who thought the whole affair had been rubbish anyway! People who don't approve of the monarchy had their televisions and radios switched off all day, held alternative parties, and even went on coach trips 'to places where the royal family can't reach'.

One group of about 100 people organized a day out by ferry to republican France, which hasn't had a monarchy for nearly 200 years. When they reached the French port of Boulougne, they drank a toast to the country's Socialist leader, François Mitterand.

Unfortunately, he couldn't be with them – he was at the wedding!

8
Memories of the Wedding Day

Everywhere in Britain people treasure special memories of how they spent the Royal Wedding Day. I asked some children to give me their memories of this very special day – and very special they are.

I can remember many memories about the Royal Wedding. My first memory is of the soldiers marching in the smart black and red uniforms and all the crowds cheering and waving flags. There were millions of people in the streets. The second memory is of the ivory silk dress. When Lady Diana went down the aisle it looked really nice. She had a long train which was twenty-five feet long and Lady Diana had a veil over her face. The third memory is of the music. It was very, very nice. It made my ears sing.

My favourite memory is when Prince Charles kissed Lady Diana on the balcony. Last of all I remember the Prince and Princess of Wales leaving the palace in their carriage with blue and silver balloons tied to the back. A sign with 'Just Married' was on the back as well.

Emma Heap, 9 years, Henley-in-Arden J&I School

7.30 a.m. Tresaith, Cardigan. We awoke to the sound of 'God Save our Gracious Queen', Mummy and Granny were crashing about the caravan getting breakfast ready. Richard and I were told to put something tidy on and to get washed. Dad was getting ready to play golf.

9.30 a.m. We arrived at Jean's bungalow having had one false start because we had to return to the caravan to collect Grannie's Souvenir Programme. There were 13 of us in the lounge watching the wedding. We had Union Jacks to wave and Grannie had made a small wedding cake. Jean supplied sherry, wine, fresh salmon sandwiches and cakes. As the procession drove through London everyone was fidgety and chattering. Mum kept saying doesn't the Prince look nervous and some of the others kept saying 'wow'. We stayed at Jean's until the Prince and Princess left on the Royal Train.

From 5.30 p.m. we began getting the barbecue ready, collecting firewood on the beach and boxes from the local post office. There were about 20 of us. We lit the fire and the mums began to cook hamburgers, eggs and sausages. We had shandy to celebrate with, and the adults had beer and wine. At about 7 p.m. we went for a swim it was absolutely gorgeous and we dried ourselves around the fire. As the adults got merrier we played around the beach with lighted torches and we ended the day singing songs around the fire. I'm sure Prince Charles and Lady Diana enjoyed their day, but so did I.

Jane Davies, 9 years, Snitterfield School

To get to St Paul's Cathedral they went by coach. On both sides were soldiers and policemen. Prince Charles wore a Navy uniform with a sword and belt. Lady Diana had a long white dress with a long train and tiara. It was a happy day.

Jo Wright, 5½ years, Henley-in-Arden J&I School

I woke at 9.30 to find the television on. Everyone seemed to be on strike. Something buzzed at the back of my mind. The Royal Wedding. I leapt out of bed leaving the dog covered in sheets and blankets. Nothing had happened to the television yet except a reporter was interviewing people who had slept on the pavement.

The first to come in view on our screen was the Queen in her green dress. About two hours later Chris came round from next door to see the Royal Wedding on our colour set.

When Lady Diana appeared we all said how lovely she was and how nice the bridesmaids were. One of the highlights was when Lady Diana got Prince Charles' name wrong.

The bit I enjoyed most was the kiss, but of course Mummy missed it for she was getting drinks in the kitchen.

Our pudding at teatime was brought round by the vet next door. It had a Union Jack made out of cream on the top that was pink, white and green. It also had sponge that contained alcohol.

Everyone got very merry after toasting the couple many times with homemade wine.

Rachel Barlow, 10 years, Snitterfield School

It was eleven o'clock July 29th 1981. I got my mum and told her the Royal wedding had started on the TV.

We saw the wedding and the best bit I think was the coachmen. They were special police with guns. Not many people knew that.

Ian Tonner, 9 years, Henley-in-Arden J&I School

I can remember all the crowds cheering when the Princess Diana and the Earl Spencer left Clarence House on their way to St Paul's Cathedral.

Another thing was when Diana and Charles made their mistakes. Diana's was 'Philip, Charles, Arthur George' instead of 'Charles, Philip, Arthur, George' and Charles said 'and with all my goods' instead of 'and with all my worldly goods'.

Another thing I remember is the bridesmaids' dresses made of silk. The happiest part was when Charles and Diana kissed on the Royal balcony.

Marcia Robbins, 10 years, Henley-in-Arden J&I School

On the day of the Royal Wedding everyone was happy and I remembered when they kissed on the balcony. It was a wonderful day. I liked the sword that Prince Charles wore and it was the 29th of July. Lady Diana had a very nice dress I liked it and all the crowds were cheering.

Fleur Astbury, 6 years, Henley-in-Arden J&I School

On the royal wedding day I watched it on the television. Then I went to a street party. At the street party we played records, and we all ate cake. I got up at 7.30 to watch it. When Lady Diana got out of the glass coach her dress was all wrinkled. Her dress was really

nice. I liked the part where Diana kissed Prince
Charles. Prince Charles looked nice and neat with his
uniform on. Prince Edward and Andrew looked nice
with their clothes on. The bridesmaids looked lovely
especially the two little girls. I would have loved to
have been there, outside listening to the sermon. At
the street party I had ice cream, jelly, crisps and
sweets. We played games like musical arms, tig, hide
and seek. I really enjoyed that day. I wish we could
have another like it. My mum stayed at home and
watched it on the television. My mum liked the part
where Lady Diana got out of the coach. The Queen
Mother looked nice, so did Lady Diana's mother. Then
I went home to bed.

Teresa Walsh, 11 years, St Benedict's School

The people were cheering and waving flags. They felt
happy. I remember when they kissed each other when
they got home to the palace.
Joshua Myers, 5½ years, Henley-in-Arden J&I School

When I had got dressed I switched on the television at
about 9.30 a.m. I watched it for about 30 minutes. At
10.00 a.m. I went to the field where the party was
being held. Four men had been roasting a pig since
5.00 a.m. At 11.00 a.m. I went home and watched the
wedding. I liked the bits when they got their vows
wrong. When the opera singer came on I went into my
back garden and played football until my mum said
she had finished singing.

At 1.35 p.m. I went to the field and people were
setting up the games like tossing the bail, welly wang-

ing etc. The party started at 4.00 p.m. but until then I played football and watched the T.V.

On the field all the games were free and the food was free. Some of the children had enough food to last a week. I played mostly on the pinball machine and managed to get scores in the 5000s. As the afternoon wore on the prizes were given out. The first slice of the pig came at about 6.00 p.m.

At about 7.00 p.m. there was a disco. I danced until 10.00 p.m. and then went home, tired but pleased the wedding had given us such a good time.

Andrew Bennett, 11 years, Snitterfield School

On Wednesday, 29th of July I woke up at about 7.30. I had a strange feeling of excitement, then I suddenly realised that it was the Royal Wedding. I heard voices downstairs, so I got out of bed. I went downstairs and had some toast, then went into the living room. I sat impatiently on the sofa. The Royal Wedding came on at about 10.00. I watched all the relations like the Queen arrive. Everybody seemed to be wearing blue. Probably the best moment of the day for me was when I saw the first glimpse of Lady Diana's wedding dress. It was made of cream silk. When she got out of the glass carriage my mum noticed that her dress was creased. The Earl Spencer (Lady Diana's father) led her up the aisle. I think Lady Diana has a charming voice. I thought it was funny when Lady Diana said 'Philip Charles Arthur George'. But I don't blame her because it must have been very scary knowing that there were millions of people from all over the world watching. I went to a Fancy Dress party with a pig roast. In the fancy dress I went as Titania Queen of the

Fairies like in A Midsummer Night's Dream. I wore a lace skirt, a boob tube and a pair of white sandals.

Lisa Trotman, 9 years, Snitterfield School

I asked the nurse to put on the radio on and the radio told me that Prince Charles and Lady Diana were going to be married. I heard that the coach was silver and bright.

Prince Charles had a lovely uniform and a black cap. Lady Diana had a long white dress. I was in hospital because I had a fractured hip. I had an injection. I was not allowed in the other room to watch the television because the bed was stuck on the floor.

Amardeep Nakra, 11 years,
Frederick Bird Junior School

On Wednesday 29th July I was so happy because it was the Royal Wedding. I liked Lady Di's dress and Prince Charles' uniform. Lots and lots of people came to the wedding. Afterwards my eyes were hurting me.

Then we had got ready lots of Indian food, and we had lots of other things for the party. We had cake and drinks.

Ranjit Gheent Kaur, 10 years,
Frederick Bird Junior School

I liked the bit when they kissed each other. That made me feel sort of funny. I remember when they went into church and walked by the chairs up the aisle.

Jamie Houghton, 5 years, Henley-in-Arden School

9
Wedding Gifts

From the moment the forthcoming marriage was announced, presents began arriving at Buckingham Palace in their hundreds. The task of supervising and cataloguing them all was given to Rear Admiral Sir Hugh Janion, and he kept them all in the private cinema at the Palace.

Everything from sweets and pocket-money from children, through handiwork lovingly made by pensioners, to exotic and opulent gifts from foreign Heads of State rolled in.

On the wishes of the couple, details were not disclosed about the gifts they received from the royal family.

However, by tradition, Prince Charles should have been able to give Diana an extremely valuable set of emeralds as a wedding gift to her. The jewels once belonged to Queen Alexandra and, according to her wish, they were to be handed down forever to future Queens of England as a marriage gift. However, the last time these stunning jewels were seen in public was round the neck of Queen Mary, and what's happened to them since is a bit of a mystery.

There are rumours that Queen Mary handed them to her son, who briefly became King – Edward the

Eighth – more than forty years ago. He gave up the throne because he had fallen in love with a divorced American, Mrs Wallis Simpson. This led to a great crisis, and Edward had to choose between the Crown and marrying Mrs Simpson. He chose Mrs Simpson, and his younger brother became King George the Sixth, Charles's grandfather.

Later, Edward married Mrs Simpson and they became the Duke and Duchess of Windsor. If Edward did give Queen Alexandra's emeralds to his bride, it's unlikely anyone will know until after the Duchess's death.

As wedding presents for Charles and Diana from guests and the public arrived, a selection of them were put on public display at St James's Palace a few days after the wedding.

Here's just a few of these: From the Foreign Diplomatic Corps (more than 150 embassies made contributions) – a bed.

From New Zealand – all wool carpets.

From Julia-Ann Chalmers, aged seven – a 20p postal order so the couple could buy their own gift, plus the offer to make some table mats. The Palace replied that the mats would be very welcome.

From the staff of a mid-Wales joinery – an oak Welsh dresser.

From Canterbury Cathedral – a paperweight made from a piece of fifteenth-century Caen stone removed during restoration work on the cathedral.

From the Northern Ireland linen industry – thirty pairs of plain double white sheets, tablecloths and matching napkins in embroidered damask, tray cloths, satin-bound towels, towelling face cloths, six dozen hankies and six-dozen man-size ones!

From Canada – an antique Canadian bedroom suite including a four-poster bed made from maplewood.

From Sir Harry Secombe – a cardboard cut-out of Battersea Power Station (jokes about cardboard cut-outs were a feature of the radio 'Goon Show' which Sir Harry starred in, and Charles loved) and a pair of portable cassette recorders with headphones.

From Greater Manchester Council – three engineering apprenticeships for unemployed young people.

From Councillor Vernon Goold – a nickel-silver mousetrap.

From President and Mrs Reagan of the United States – a Steuben glass bowl and a handmade porcelain centrepiece.

From the Royal Hospital, Chelsea – a silver statuette of a Chelsea Pensioner.

From the Lord Lieutenant of Lancashire – cast-iron fire dogs made by a Lancashire blacksmith whose trademark is a ram's head. As a special feature, he hammered a wink into one of the ram's eyes.

From pupils and old girls of West Heath School (where Diana went) – a handbound copy of the Book of Common Prayer and a pair of silver salt-cellars.

From the King and Queen of Tonga – a handmade bedspread made by the Queen herself, two clothes stands, two black leather saddles for Charles, and black coral jewellery for Diana.

From the Young England Kindergarten – a collage of the Royal Firework Display.

From the staff of Dartmoor Prison – a ball and chain which can be used as a paperweight.

From a group of millionaires in Oklahoma City in

the United States – part share in an oil well, said to be worth £25,000 a month. The Palace had to turn this down, because it was felt it wouldn't be right to accept an income from a foreign country.

From the Cabinet – a pair of eighteenth-century candlesticks.

From South Africa – a silver salver with a decorative border in gold of protea, the country's national flower.

From physically handicapped children at a school in Sussex – homegrown myrtle for the bride's bouquet.

From Australia – twenty handcrafted silver platters.

From the American Ambassador, John J. Louis – a small oil painting by American artist Henry Kohler of Charles playing polo.

From Bahrain – a solid gold, two-foot model of a dhow – the Arab sailing ship.

From the United Arab Emirates – a stunning collection of jewelled watches, bracelets, necklaces, and brooches.

From Greater London Council – a 1933 watercolour of Covent Garden.

From the King and Queen of Spain – a set of hide suitcases.

From Spike Milligan, another 'Goon' – a poem, and a wooden box with copper pieces on each end that give off a mild electric shock.

From Amanda and Melanie – a heart-shaped shrivelled potato.

From Tommy McKay, a blind and disabled Londoner – a grandmother clock he made.

From Joanne and Clare Harrison – blue and pink toothbrushes.

From the crew of HMS *Bronington* (Charles used to be her skipper) – a model of the ship.

From the Japanese royal family – lacquer work and gold-painted plate.

From Clementine Hambro, one of the bridesmaids – bathrobes with Charles and Diana embroidered on the back.

From the people of Jersey – two cows.

At six o'clock on the morning of the first day of the exhibition at St James's Palace, 300 people were in the queue – four hours before the doors opened. By noon, the queue had swelled to 4000, and it stretched from St James's, down Marlborough Road, turned right into The Mall, past Clarence House, Lancaster House and Buckingham Palace, and then turned round and came all the way back.

Entrance fee was £1.50 for adults, 80 pence for children and 70 pence for pensioners . . . and all the proceeds went to charity. In all, some 1200 presents were picked to put on show, and they were insured for £250 thousand. It must have been a very difficult task to decide which ones should be displayed – though with some, the decision was easy. For example, the stone table given by the King of Swaziland in Africa was so heavy that officials feared it might crash through the floor – so that was left out!

Outside, the temperature soared to 87°F, but that didn't deter the queuers. There were many stories of families who'd left home at the crack of dawn to see the presents. Some who hadn't been able to be on the streets for the wedding wanted to make up for what they'd missed by admiring the gifts. One lady, a Mrs

Binstead, had paid £600 for a return air ticket from Hong Kong just to see the presents. Others, who had been amongst the crowds on the big day, wanted to complete the great occasion by going round the exhibition.

Three thousand people a day saw the display and unfortunately – though understandably – they didn't move as quickly as the officials would have liked. So some had to queue for up to six hours, and at the end of each day disappointed people had to be turned away. But so many feet walked over the covers that had been laid down to protect the beautiful carpets that they had to be replaced three times.

There was plenty to amaze, astound, impress and amuse the public as they slowly wandered through the display area. Most popular item of all, of course, was the wedding dress – on show with a bridesmaid's dress and a pageboy outfit. There was a nineteenth-century square piano, a Broadwood grand piano, and an electronic organ painted in military green and battleship grey. There were soft toys – a white fur rabbit with silk bow tie, a black cat for good luck, and two mice dolls in wedding dress. Some thoughtful person had given them a library-ladder for reaching the top shelves of their bookcases.

There were vacuum cleaners, automatic tea-makers, and a microwave oven – the kind of gifts that most young couples hope to get as wedding gifts, but in the case of Charles and Diana, these presents are likely to be of more use to their staff at Highgrove.

Other things that caught the eye were masses of handknitted tea cosies, a set of door chimes that played twenty-four different musical welcomes, silk carpets, a wind-surfing board for the action-man Prince, a silver thimble, a box of toffees, a glue pen, a Rubik cube, a Matt Monroe record, a dog basket, a tiny hand-knitted bee, lots of sporting gifts and picnic hampers – all of them getting as much attention from the public as the glittering jewels given by Arab countries.

The exhibition was expensive to put on. Security was tight, with officials keeping a careful eye on the fabulously expensive gifts and commissionaires keeping watch on the crowds. But when it was over, £85,000 had been raised – and that, combined with profits from the sale of official wedding souvenirs, meant that organizations which help the handicapped were better off by £750,000 – a fine gesture during the International Year of Disabled People.

The exhibition closed on 4 October, but a smaller one of 200 presents and *the* dress began touring the country, so that people who weren't able to travel to London could have the chance to see them.

The presents that didn't go 'on tour' began arriving at Highgrove on 15 October.

It was a hush-hush operation, and the removal firm only got to know about the job a few days beforehand. A team of twelve, specially trained in packaging and transporting antiques and other delicate treasures, spent three days packing up a selection of gifts.

Then, two massive vans set off for Gloucestershire, with a police escort and a small group of local people gathered outside the gates of Highgrove to watch them arrive. The stunning array of presents that had been on show for everyone to see had finally become the private possessions of Charles and Diana.

10

The Honeymoon

Everyone loves a guessing game, and in the early summer of 1981, the nation and its newspapers were joining in the great game of trying to guess where Charles and Diana would go for their honeymoon. The names of some of the world's most romantic places were put forward, but the only ones who knew were the couple themselves and their staff who were making the arrangements.

Would it be the Caribbean, those lovely islands off the east coast of America? The people of St Kitts-Nevis, one of the Caribbean's most idyllic spots, said the honeymooners would be most welcome. Back home, some people remembered there'd been complaints from certain quarters when Princess Anne and Captain Mark Philips had visited that part of the world on their honeymoon. Such a long voyage in the royal yacht, *Britannia*, means that a tanker has to be there as well to refuel her, and that adds to the cost.

Princess Margaret, who often visits the Caribbean, gave a good tip when she attended a ceremony to launch an issue of stamps for the island of Nevis featuring the royal yacht. She very sensibly pointed out that the more people talked about a place, the less likely Charles and Diana were to visit it.

From Africa came an invitation from the Ashanti people of central Ghana to spend the honeymoon with them. Reporters thought they might be on the right track when the manager of an hotel on the lovely Adriatic island of Sveti Stefen claimed that a special cottage there was being prepared for the Prince and Princess.

Bearing Princess Margaret's words in mind, that cottage never stood a chance of the honeymooners stepping through its doors.

It's only in recent years that members of the royal family have travelled abroad for their honeymoons. Queen Victoria, for example, spent a three-day holiday at Windsor Castle after her wedding and even then she spent a lot of time dealing with important papers and affairs of state. Her son, Edward, Prince of Wales, spent a week's honeymoon at Osborne, the Queen's house on the Isle of Wight. The present Queen Mother and her husband, who later became King George the Sixth, spent the first part of their honeymoon in a country house in Surrey, and then went to Glamis Castle in Scotland. And the Queen and Prince Philip began their honeymoon at Broadlands, the fine house in Hampshire belonging to Lord and Lady Mountbatten, and then travelled to the Balmoral estate.

The guessing game about Charles and Diana's destinations ended on 21 July with the announcement that they, too, would start their honeymoon at Broadlands, and then fly to Gibraltar to join *Britannia*, which would take them on a Mediterranean cruise. There had been a few clues about Broadlands – the house was to be closed to the public during the week of the wedding, and Charles and Diana were leaving London from Waterloo, the main line station that serves Hampshire.

On the day, the couple arrived at the station in the horse-drawn coach with the 'Just Married' sign on the back. Diana had kisses for the two men who had masterminded the wedding plans: Lord MacLean, the Queen's Lord Chamberlain, and Sir John Johnston, Comptroller of the Lord Chamberlain's office.

Then, they stepped into an observation car at the back of an ordinary diesel train – though it had no ordinary, fare-paying passengers! – and set off on the journey to Romsey, the nearest station to Broadlands. Diana looked lovely in a peach-coloured dress and short sleeved bolero, and in her hat were ostrich feathers. In the royal compartment of the train were two marvellous arrangements of flowers, a bowl of fruit and a silver tea service.

The train arrived at Romsey at four minutes past six, having been shadowed all the way by a police helicopter. Station manager John Spiers greeted the couple, and the whole town was there to cheer and wave. The abbey bells pealed, and bunting was everywhere.

It was just a short drive to Broadlands, and once the big gates closed behind the newlyweds, everything was done to make their stay there very private. The sixty-room mansion, which now belongs to Lord Mountbatten's son, Lord Romsey, his 6000 acres of ground – and it was a perfect place for Charles and Dianao to get some peace after the endless sound of cheering since early morning.

Policemen, some with dogs, patrolled the estate – always keeping a discreet distance. But that didn't stop reporters getting their stories, and they said that Charles and Diana had been spotted the next morning, strolling hand-in-hand across the lawns. The river Test flows through the grounds, and it provides some of the best salmon fishing in the country. Charles went fishing for a few hours on their second evening there, on his own, but he didn't catch anything!

In the town, crowds flocked to the abbey to see the grave of Charles's beloved great-uncle Lord Mountbatten because rumour had it that Diana's bouquet had been placed there. Such is rumour – in fact, it had been placed on the Tomb of the Unknown Soldier in Westminster Abbey.

The weather was glorious for the brief stay at Broadlands. The police threw out one press photographer who managed to get within 450 yards of the house by crawling through the undergrowth. But they looked more kindly on a letter handed to them at one of the gates by seven-year-old Marcus Cass. It read: 'Dear Prince Charles and Lady Diana. I came to Romsey to see you but people kept pushing, so I wasn't able to see you. Mummy said just cheer when other people cheer, so we did. I hope you are a happy family.'

The couple stayed at Broadlands from Wednesday evening until Saturday morning, when they left by car for Eastleigh Airport at Southampton where an RAF Andover aircraft was waiting to fly them to Gibraltar, with one stop at Oporto in Portugal for refuelling. Jet airliners take only three hours to reach Gibraltar, but the Andover is smaller and slower, and the journey took much longer.

The Andover landed at Gibraltar just before five in

the evening, with Charles at the controls. One newspaper reported that, during the flight, Diana had tidied up the cabin after a meal and got out the vacuum cleaner! Who knows! After being greeted by local dignitaries, they drove through the streets to the harbour in the only open-top car in Gibraltar.

As you know Gibraltar, with its famous Rock, is a small headland right on the southern tip of Spain. It's of vital importance because it guards the narrowish entrance into the Mediterranean Sea from the Atlantic Ocean. For many years, Gibraltar has been ruled by Britain and it looks very British – even the policemen wear the same uniforms as our 'bobbies'.

But Spain has always claimed that Gibraltar rightly belongs to her. It's a very touchy issue between the two countries. For a long time, Spain closed the border, and it's only just been opened again. The political bosses in Madrid, the Spanish capital, get very angry when Britain does something which seems to strengthen the fact that Gibraltar is British – so imagine how they felt when the news broke that Charles and Diana were going there during their honeymoon.

The reaction was strong. King Juan Carlos and Queen Sophia of Spain turned down their invitation to the wedding – very much a political move because they are close friends of the British royal family. Spain suggested that the royal yacht could sail from one of her ports, to take the heat out of the situation – but plans went ahead for Charles and Diana to meet *Britannia* at Gibraltar.

The Gibraltarians were delighted. It gave them a very dramatic way to show that the little colony wanted to stay British. As Charles and Diana drove through the streets, banners proclaimed: 'British we are and British we stay.'

People were hanging out of windows, cheering and waving, and bunting decked every house. It was the first royal visit there since 1954, and the locals put on a tremendous display of patriotism.

As the yacht pulled out of the harbour, Charles and Diana came out on to the deck, holding hands. Pink flares shot into the sky, and a military band on the wharf played Rod Stewart's song 'Sailing'. Between 300 and 400 small boats escorted *Britannia* out of the harbour, blaring their hooters. The sound was deafening. Slowly, the *Britannia* gained distance on them and literally sailed off into the sunset.

The *Britannia* is a floating palace, and the royal apartments are sumptuous. The state rooms are big enough to entertain dozens of important guests during royal trips. There are four master bedrooms with magnificent bathrooms; fine linen sheets that were made for Queen Victoria, exquisite cutlery, china, and glassware, an open-air swimming pool, and even a black Rolls-Royce in the hold. She was built on Clydeside in Scotland in 1952 and launched a year later – the year of the Queen's Coronation. She cost £2 million, and it now costs almost as much as that every year to keep her sailing. *Britannia* has a crew of 22 officers and 254 men – and for the next few days, they somehow managed to make their ship 'disappear' in the vastness of the Mediterranean. Try as they might, with their high-speed boats and aeroplanes, the press could not track her down.

On 7 August, the yacht arrived at the Greek island of Ithica – home of the legendary hero, Odysseus. There,

HAPPINESS: The bride and groom in this picture by Lord Snowdon to mark their engagement. The engagement ring is an oval sapphire surrounded by fourteen diamonds.
WELCOME HOME!: Prince Charles's golden labrador, Harvey, greets his master at Balmoral. The Prince joined Lady Diana there after his tour of New Zealand, Australia, Venezuela and the United States.

THAT OTHER DRESS!: Lady Diana wears a low-cut evening dress on her first official appearance with Prince Charles after their engagement — a charity performance at Goldsmiths' Hall, London.

A KISS FOR MY LADY: Schoolboy Nicholas Hardy shows his gallantry to Lady Diana during a visit to Gloucester in March 1981.

OFF TO THE RACES: Prince Charles and Lady Diana ride in an open carriage on the first day of the Royal Ascot race meeting in June 1981.

FACING THE CAMERAS TOGETHER: Answering questions during a television interview recorded at Buckingham Palace which was shown on the eve of their wedding.

GOLDEN DAY: Lady Diana in the glass coach on her way to St Paul's Cathedral – and for the world, a first glimpse of her dress.
PRINCE AND PRINCESS: Charles and his bride descend the steps of St Paul's after their marriage, with the Princess's train sweeping twenty-five feet behind her.

ON THE BALCONY: The bride and groom, joined by the pages, three of the bridesmaids, Prince Philip, the Queen Mother and the Queen on the balcony of Buckingham Palace. Down below, half a million people cheered.

THE KISS: The Prince and Princess of Wales kiss on the balcony of Buckingham Palace.

THE WEDDING GROUP: Taken by Patrick Lichfield at Buckingham Palace as soon as everyone returned from the cathedral. (See end page for list of names.)

PRESENTS GALORE: Gifts given by the public to the Prince and Princess – including children's paintings, soft toys, even a pair of toothbrushes – went on show in St James's Palace a week after the wedding.

BACK HOME: The Prince and Princess leave the RAF VC-10 aircraft that flew them home to Scotland from Egypt at the end of their overseas honeymoon.

THIS IS HOME: Highgrove, the Georgian mansion near Tetbury in Gloucestershire where the Prince and Princess will have their main home.

ROAMIN' IN THE GLOAMIN': The Prince and Princess walk hand in hand along the riverbank at Balmoral. They continued their honeymoon in Scotland at the end of a two-week cruise in the Mediterranean.

WHAT'S YOUR NAME?: The Princess makes a special point of talking to children during her walkabouts. Here she meets one of the young citizens of Chesterfield in Derbyshire, on level terms!

Charles and Diana went swimming in a sheltered cove
– and very soon prying helicopters were hovering
above. So the Greek air force issued a warning to all
unwelcome pilots – stay clear of the *Britannia* or we'll
send our jets after you!

The royal couple had to abandon plans for sight-
seeing – and for extra protection, a Greek Navy gun-
boat shadowed the *Britannia*. The yacht sailed on,
anchoring off the spectacular island of Santorini – the
rim of a volcano that disappeared under the sea
thousands of years ago. The cruise lasted for twelve
days – nearly all of it in total privacy – before *Britannia*
put in at Port Said in Egypt, at the top of the Suez
Canal.

The couple appeared on deck, looking sun-tanned,
and Diana wore a straw hat, white blouse and blue
culottes. In the evening, two distinguished guests
arrived for dinner: President Sadat of Egypt and his
wife. Only two months later, the president was killed
by assassins – and Prince Charles returned to Egypt to
walk through the streets of Cairo in his funeral procession. But on that night, there was no hint of the
tragedy to come. Fireworks lit up the night sky, bands
played barely recognizable versions of 'God Save the
Queen', and the president awarded Prince Charles
with the Order of the Republic, First Class, one of
Egypt's highest decorations.

Next day, *Britannia* paid a toll of £7900 to pass
through the Suez Canal – the impressive waterway
that cuts straight through the Egyptian desert to link
the Mediterranean with the Red Sea. The cruise was
coming to an end, and after a final day of relaxation
and sunbathing, the Prince and Princess flew home

from Hurghada on the Red Sea on 15 August. President and Mrs Sadat were there to see them off.

The aircraft landed at Lossiemouth in Morayshire. Charles took the wheel of a blue Granada estate, the back loaded with presents, and drove Diana to Balmoral for the final part of their honeymoon.

Photographers were invited one day to take pictures of the healthy, happy, tanned couple – and Diana told them that she could 'highly recommend' married life!

I I
The Visit to Wales

What a welcome was waiting in the hills and valleys of Wales when Charles took his bride to the Principality three months after their wedding. For Diana, it was her first official royal tour, and her first visit to Wales. During much of the three days, the weather was dreadful, but the people of Wales ignored the rain – and so did their Prince and Princess.

From the outset, it was clear who the crowds had come to see. Diana captured hearts wherever she went and when a massed choir sang 'God Bless the Prince of Wales' they added a final line – 'God bless his Princess, too'.

The tour took them through all eight counties, from the peaks of Snowdonia to the beaches of Pembrokeshire and the hills of mid-Wales, some 400 miles in all, travelling by royal train and by car. Accompanying Diana for the first time was her new lady-in-waiting, Miss Anne Beckwith-Smith.

On the eve of the visit, on Monday, 26 October, a bomb was found in the town of Pontypridd, where Charles and Diana were due on the Thursday. It was later claimed to be the work of a nationalist group, the Workers Army of the Welsh Republic, which doesn't want the country to have any royal connections. Despite the increased tension caused by this incident, it didn't stem the great swell of affection for the couple from the vast majority of Welsh people.

The first day set the style for the tour, with walk-abouts in every place they visited. Diana was wearing an outfit in bottle green and red, no doubt carefully chosen to reflect the colours of the Welsh flag. She chatted easily with everyone she met and seemed to make a bee-line for the elderly, the young and the handicapped. Experienced reporters of the royal scene remarked how incomplete Charles seemed to be when Diana was not by his side.

There were a few little hitches, often amusing – like the time when Charles stepped out of the Rolls at a place called Buckley and said how glad he was to be in Shotton!

In Rhyl, crowds had been waiting for more than three hours to catch a glimpse of them. Bands played familiar anthems like 'Men of Harlech', and the crowd showed the warmth of their feeling by bursting into song with 'We'll Keep a Welcome in the Hillsides'. One store sold out of light-weight aluminium ladders – bought by people at the back of the crowd, so they could get a better view!

As the couple headed through north Wales, with Diana collecting bouquet after bouquet, there were cheering people on every corner. All police leave had been cancelled as every man was needed for crowd duties, and schools had been given the day off.

Seven-year-old Simon Edwin will never forget what happened to him that day at the Dees-side Leisure Centre. He'd been waiting patiently at the barriers, and when the Princess came close to him, Simon said quite boldly to her: 'My dad says "give us a kiss"!' Diana laughed, and said: 'Well, you'd better give me one.' Then she bent down, and kissed Simon on the cheek. She also met eight-year-old Joanne Edwards, who suffers from the crippling disease spina bifida. Diana half-lifted Joanna out of her wheelchair to give her a big hug.

The visit to Bangor was slightly marred by student demonstrators chanting: 'Go home, Charles; go home, English Princess.' And at Caernarvon, a young woman broke free from the crowds and sprayed paint on the royal car. She was soon hustled away, and later fined £25.

Caernarvon was, of course, the scene of Charles's Investiture as Prince of Wales in 1969. A few days before this visit, a letter had been received saying: 'We will not forget 1969 – beware Caernarvon.' But Charles and Diana took no notice, and when they spotted a group of protestors, they went over to them and simply smiled. It was a tense moment for the security men.

At Caernarvon, they were greeted by Lord Snowdon, the constable of the castle and the man who'd made all the arrangements for the Investiture. Inside the grounds of the thirteenth-century castle, they sat on two raised chairs in a freezing wind and listened to children singing a song about the animals going into the ark two by two – and it went on a long time!

On the second day of the visit, the heavens opened and torrential rain came down for most of the day. But it didn't dampen the spirits, and the drenched crowds stood and waited. Diana wore a biscuit-coloured coat and skirt and a chic hat with an ostrich feather and net.

As the day wore on, and the rain came down, the decoration on the hat looked less and less jaunty and more and more droopy! In the tiny city of St David's – it's named after the country's patron saint and just 1500 people live there – Charles and Diana attended a service to mark the 800th anniversary of the cathedral. The bells rang out, and hundreds of people who waited outside because the cathedral was full heard the service over loudspeakers, with Prince Charles reading the Lesson.

It was another day packed full with events, and once again, Diana paid most attention to children and old people. She was presented with a small doll dressed in full Welsh costume, and moments later spotted four-year-old Ruth Devonald wearing the same clothes. 'Look,' said Diana to the little girl, 'I have a miniature version of you.' And she seemed really thrilled to meet one of her namesakes, Diana Evans aged two months, when her mother proudly showed the baby to the Princess.

Meanwhile, Charles and Anne Beckwith-Smith were being heaped with presents for Diana. Thirteen-year-old Penny Golightly gave Prince Charles a poem entitled 'A Ballad to Lady Diana', and asked if he'd be kind enough to pass it to his wife. Charles said he would, adding: 'I'm used to collecting things for her now, as you can see. Thank you.'

When they arrived, ten minutes late, at Haverford-west the rain was falling heavily and the wind was blowing, but they were determined not to disappoint everyone who'd been waiting, so they carried on with their planned walkabout. At one point, Charles was obviously worried that Diana – walking round with no protection from the rain – would get thoroughly soaked. 'Darling, don't walk out in the rain,' he told her. 'You'll get so wet.' Then he took a brolly from the lady-in-waiting, and held it over her head. And Diana carried on – wearing no gloves, despite the cold, so her hands would be free to shake all the many others, big and small, that stretched out to greet her.

By the time they reached Carmarthen, four police women were needed to carry all the presents. Lots of people in the crowds were holding Charles and Diana balloons, which they'd no doubt been keeping since the wedding day. Anyone who didn't have a balloon could easily buy one, though, from the team of London street-traders who were enterprisingly selling their wedding leftovers, just a few steps ahead of the couple throughout the tour.

The next stop was at Llandeilo, a place well-known for its strong Welsh nationalist feelings. It was here that the last Welsh Prince of Wales, Llewellyn, was killed in 1282 in a battle against King Edward the First of England. In these modern times, unemployment is the biggest worry in Llandeilo. But the royal visit brightened up the bleak prospects on this rainy day, and Charles and Diana put aside their umbrellas so that the locals could get a better view of them. 'Are you sodden wet?' Charles asked a group of youngsters. 'It's one of those days when I'm glad I'm not at sea!'

Another group complained to him that they couldn't see Diana, who was walking along a line of people on the other side of the street. 'I'm sorry, there is only one of her,' he said with a smile. 'I haven't got enough wives to go round.' And from time to time, he found himself apologizing to townsfolk saying: 'I'm sorry, you'll have to make do with me, instead!' Then, it was out of the rain for the drive to Swansea, where in the evening they attended a gala concert.

The third and final day of the visit began at the Royal Welsh showground at Llanelwedd. Among the gifts they received there was a pair of leather armchairs, a mountain ewe called Fedw Suis and a black, award-winning Welsh heifer called Sandra.

Then, during a trip round the maternity ward at Llwynypia Hospital, Charles said something which started the press guessing. While he was chatting to Mrs Shirley Bowen about the birth of her baby, he said he thought it was a good thing for fathers to be present when a baby is born. Could this be a hint, thought the reporters, that a royal baby might be on the way? They got their answer a few days later!

The Princess also had a word with Mrs Bowen, and with everyone else in the maternity ward, where every cot had been specially decorated for the occasion. Then, the couple popped into the men's orthopaedic ward.

All the way from Treherbert to Pontypridd, a ten-mile drive through the industrial heartland of Wales, crowds lined the route.

Cardiff was the grand finale of the tour. In a special ceremony, Diana was granted the freedom of the city – only the second woman to receive the honour. The first was her mother-in-law, the Queen. For the ceremony, Diana changed from a suit of burgundy velvet into a knee-length blue chiffon dress with bat-wing sleeves under a black velvet coat.

During her marriage vows she had not sworn to obey her husband, but on this occasion she had to swear an oath to be obedient to the Lord Mayor of Cardiff – to 'obey his Warrants, Precepts and Commands'. She was presented with a scroll in a silver casket, and made her first official speech in Welsh. She said: 'It's a great pleasure to come to Wales. I hope to come here again, soon. I'm glad to be the Princess of such a wonderful place.'

By any standards, the tour had been a great success. The Prince of Wales had personally shown his bride, and their Princess, to the people of Wales. Diana had passed with distinction her first real test on a royal tour. The choir that sang 'God Bless the Prince of Wales' really did echo the feelings of the Welsh people when they added that final line – 'God Bless his Princess, too.'

12

Visit of the Snow Princess

It was a very special morning for the 320 children of Tetbury junior school when the Princess of Wales came to visit. It's one of three schools in the small Gloucestershire town – there's also an infants and a comprehensive – and it happens to be just down the road from Highgrove.

When the engagement was announced, some of the juniors wrote messages of congratulations to Charles and Diana, and the headmaster added a note saying that should the royal couple ever want to make a quiet, private visit to their local school, they would be more than welcome.

During the summer holidays came a reply – the Princess would love to meet the children on 8 December. When the day came, the first winter snow was thick on the ground, but that didn't put the Princess off. She drove the mile or so to the school from Highgrove at the wheel of her silver Ford Escort, and scores of photographers were there to see her arrive. Reporters quickly called her 'The Snow Princess'.

Once inside the school doors, it became a private visit. The press were not allowed in, though later cameramen were invited to take pictures of a presentation, when the Princess was given, among other things, an inscribed glass paperweight made by a local craftsman, Fred Beanes.

The Princess was shown round the school by the headmaster, Mr Des Carwardine. She admired all the Christmas decorations made by the children, and the nativity scene in the entrance hall.

During the two and a half hours she was at the school, she spoke to every child and went into all eleven classrooms. Lessons in English, maths and nature studies went on as normally as possible while the Princess talked to pupils about their work and their lives.

'She was marvellous,' Mr Carwardine told me afterwards, 'and very interested in everything that was happening. It was a great honour for the school.'

On her tour, Diana accidentally missed a group of children working in a corner. When this was gently pointed out to her, she went over to them straightaway and apologized! As she was leaving, she thanked everyone for the trouble they had gone to, and said she hoped to see them all again.

Later, I asked some of the children at the school to write down their memories of that day. Here are some of them:

When we were told we were to have a visit from the Princess of Wales on 8 December, everyone was very excited. I couldn't believe it as I like the Royal Family very much. Everyone was set at making this occasion one to remember. We started making Christmas decorations earlier than usual so they would be ready in time for the visit. The first decorations we made were gift boxes. The classroom gradually started to look festive. I was asked by my teacher if I would like to make a calendar. I was thrilled to bits. The calendar would have twelve little pictures, one for each month of the year. Two of the pictures would be personal to her, a baby in June and a bottle of champagne and glasses which would mark their first wedding anniversary. I thought to myself, 'Just think! My calendar will be hanging up in Highgrove House!'

The days got nearer. Photographers flooded in wanting to take pictures of us. A few days before, two men from a local paper *The Citizen* came into our classroom while we were doing practical maths. They chatted to my teacher, Miss Walker. My teacher told them I was going to give her a calendar. They asked me if they could take some pictures of me. Of course I agreed. I had never been in a paper before. I stood by the blackboard with my calendar staring at the rest of the children. I could see they were jealous.

That same days lots of men from H.T.V. came to film us having a last practice before the visit of the carols we were to sing which were: 'Oh Come All Ye Faithful' and 'While Shepherds Watched'. Big lights shone on us very brightly while we played our recorders. We could not see our music that well. That night we played on T.V.

At last the Royal day came. I made a special effort to look smart and tidy. I arrived early in my warm coat, hat, gloves and wellies as it had snowed quite deeply. When I arrived I put my trainers on and got my recorder and music ready for assembly. They were all nervewracking moments when we were waiting to go for assembly. The children came in while we played

'Unto Us a Boy is Born'. All the teachers came in looking smart in their nice clothes. Mr Bird gave us a short talk on legends. While he was talking my knees were knocking. I was excited. She came in accompanied by Mrs Cole and the vicar. She was wearing a long red coat and a brown dress. I thought she looked lovely. She had a very pretty face. At the end of assembly we played 'Silent Night'. After that we all walked out smartly. When we got to the classroom, my precious calendar was placed by the place I was sitting. I had to do painting when she came in.

I shall always remember those long nervewracking moments before she came in.

She walked through the door. She talked to my teacher. My teacher curtseyed. She walked to the first table and talked to the children there. Then she walked over to our table. 'My big moment has come' I thought to myself. I stood up and said my little speech, but before I could finish she started saying, 'Thank you very much. It's lovely.' I blushed. She said 'Which is the baby in the cot, a boy or a girl? I said I didn't know – a bit of both.' She walked around to the other tables, still holding her calendar now. When she walked out of the door we all waited until it was time to flood onto the playing field to wave goodbye. When she came out Anna Weaver and Stephen Woodburn gave her a paperweight. When she drove off slowly waving to us, I noticed that she had a Kermit the Frog mascot on her car. I thought everything was over then, but I was wrong. A group of us were interviewed with Andrew Harvey from Points West. We were on T.V. again that night.

Amanda Grant, 12 years, St Mary's C of E Junior School

I was very excited when I read that Lady Diana and Prince Charles were buying Highgrove near Tetbury. Soon they were making appearances in and around Tetbury and were invited to open an extension to the Tetbury hospital. All the children were asked to line the route of the Royal couple. I had the choice to go with the Brownies or the school. I chose to go with the Brownies. I ticked off the days on my calendar until at last the day of the visit came.

It was a warm day and the sun was shining. We had to meet outside our Brownie meeting place at 8.15. At 8.00 I left the house and called at my friend's house. It was 8.15 when we got to the meeting place. There were already lots of people there smartly dressed in their brown uniforms holding Union Jacks. We were lining Fox Hill. Already there were a few spectators standing behind the ropes. We had a long wait ahead of us because the Prince and Princess of Wales weren't coming until 10.30 a.m.

At last I saw the crowd of people coming down the hill. Among them was the Royal couple. The Princess of Wales was wearing a red top and skirt with a red and white spotted scarf. When the crowd got near us, we all started waving our flags and cheering. There was a clicking of cameras, and I just managed to catch a glimpse of Lady Diana's red suit. Then they carried on up the hill. We waited until the Royal couple came back from the hospital in their cars. Again we waved and cheered for all we were worth until the cars were out of sight. After it was all over, I felt rather flat.

The next important thing was the wedding. I sat glued to the television all morning, so did my mum. She cried at the hymns and we didn't have dinner until about half past one. That afternoon we went up to the recreation ground. There was a party commemorating the wedding, there was a band and a roundabout. Also there were races. We watched the races and then we tried to break a record. We had an enormous parcel wrapped in wallpaper. Then we got as many people as we could and played pass the parcel. Then they lit the bonfire. It was enormous. But it got out of control and set fire to the hedge, so we had to send for the fire brigade. The fire was soon put out. So that the party would carry on longer, a group came to sing for us. They came from Tetbury and were called Cheverolet. They sang songs about Lady Diana and Prince Charles. The grown-ups had champagne and had a toast to the happiness of the royal couple. The music went on into the night and was still going when I left at 11.00.

The people in the fourth year at my school wrote letters to the Prince and Princess of Wales thanking them for coming to open the extension on the hospital. With it Mr Carwardine (our headmaster) sent a letter asking if the Prince and Princess of Wales would like to come and visit us. He got back a letter saying the Princess of Wales would be very glad to come, and would it be all right for her to come on December 8th. Mr Carwardine said it would be all right and we looked forward to the day very much.

One day a couple of weeks before December 8th, we were told we had to vote for one boy and one girl who we would like to present a paperweight to the Princess of Wales. I chose my best friend Rebecca Whitlock for the girl, and who I wrote for a boy is a secret. They were collected in, and I thought no more about them.

The next day the fourth years had to stay behind and Mr Carwardine told us who had got the most votes. I hoped with all my heart I would be the girl, and I was! The boy was Stephen Woodburn. The next day we had to make up a small speech that we would have to say to the Princess of Wales. After many attempts I finally came up with one. This is it: 'Thank you very much for coming to our school to visit us. We hope we shall have the pleasure of your company again sometime in the future, and perhaps the next time Prince Charles will come with you.' We had to practise saying this to a make believe Princess of Wales (a fourth year teacher). Slowly the day of the visit came closer and closer until it was the day before. I was so nervous and excited I was sure I was going to make a mess of it and perhaps drop the glass paperweight, and I went to bed that night very excited.

I woke the next morning to find a white wilderness outside, that night it had snowed. I got dressed in a daze, wondering if it was really me who was going to present the paperweight to Princess Diana. I ate my breakfast and started off for school. I called for my friend, and we walked to school together. The Princess of Wales came in the middle of the Assembly and sat at the front of the hall. Then she made a tour of the school. I had butterflies in my stomach, and I kept repeating what I had to say until I almost forgot it. Our classroom was second from last. When the classroom door opened we all went quiet and then the Princess of Wales came in. She is much more pretty in real life than on the television. She went round the tables and spoke to people, then she came to my table. She asked Michelle Everett if her rubber was a perfumed one.

Michelle said no it wasn't, but that I had one and so she asked me if she could smell it. She then carried on looking round the classroom and then left. Now I had to act quickly. I got up and went to my teacher's desk. I picked up the box with the paperweight in, and went to wait in the cloakroom. The Princess of Wales went into one more class. I started chatting to who I think was a policeman and he was very nice to me. Then the Princess of Wales came out. With her was Stephen Woodburn. We walked behind Mr Carwardine. When we got to the door of the fourth year block, the Princess of Wales said 'What are the children behind us doing?' Mr Carwardine said that we were following them. Then the Princess asked what was in the box I was holding. Stephen told her it was a secret. When we got outside I felt really really nervous. When we got to the top of the path, I started to say my small speech and gave her the paperweight with a curtsey. All the time I felt the television cameras on us, and the cameras clicking. I was so nervous I had a nervous twitch in my cheeks. When I said to the Princess of Wales, 'Perhaps the next time Prince Charles will come with you' she said she would make him. Then she got into her car and drove off amid cheering and waving. Then I found myself being asked questions by newspaper reporters and being interviewed by cameras. That night for the first time in my life I saw myself on television. I felt very proud. I shall never forget that day as long as I live, and I don't expect the other children will either.

Anna Weaver, 11 years, St Mary's C of E Junior School

On Tuesday, 8 December, we were honoured to receive a visit from the Royal Highness the Princess of Wales.

A few weeks before the visit we were making decorations and practising two songs 'O Come All Ye Faithful' and 'While Shepherds Watched Their Flocks' and they put the tree up. Mr Carwardine, our headmaster put a message on the climbing frame. It said in Welsh 'Welcome to St Mary's Junior School, Tetbury'.

When we heard that she was coming we got ready to make our decorations and we practised the two songs nearly every day. We made gift boxes. Father Christmases, angels, windows, stars and put streamers outside in the cloak room. We also made calendars.

On December 7th the camera men came. They had four spot lights and I think four cameras. We sang the two songs and hummed 'Silent Night'. Then at about 3.00 Jonathan and I were called to put the chairs out ready for the next day.

On December 8th we all were in our school uniform, and all ready in the hall. Then Mrs Tigwell, our secretary, came and told us that she was here, so we all waited patiently. Then she came into the hall and then we all sang the two songs.

Then she went to the first year's because she wasn't coming to our class until 11.00.

When she came in the door, Miss Walker, Excell and Mrs Gates all done a fancy curtsey to her, then she went around the classroom. We were all doing different things. When it came around to me (I was making shapes out of five squares) she said 'Are you making shapes with five squares?' I said, 'Yes.' Then she said 'You couldn't make a circle.' I said 'No.'

Then she went to see the other fourth year classes.

After that they interviewed some of the people from our class. Then Anna Weaver and Stephen Woodburn presented her with a paperweight with three feathers, and engraved on it 'December 8th'. Then we all waved goodbye.

In the afternoon, Daphne Nevine came with her otter and the children in the front were told to wear their painting coats. The otter was clever but a lot of children got wet.

I liked them both in different ways.

Malcolm Wing, 11 years, St Mary's C of E Junior School

13
An Heir to the Throne

The announcement that the Princess of Wales was expecting a baby was made on 5 November 1980. When born, the child will be second in line to the throne after Charles, and the first child born to a Prince and Princess of Wales since 1905.

As the news spread, crowds gathered at London's historic Guildhall, where Charles and Diana were to be guests of the Lord Mayor for lunch. During his speech, Prince Charles spoke about their wedding day.

'We still cannot get over what happened that day,' he said. 'Neither of us can get over the atmosphere; it was electric, I felt, and so did my wife.'

The noise outside his window at Buckingham Palace had been 'almost indescribable'. Since then, he had stood at the same window trying to remember it 'so that I can tell my children what it was like. I remember several occasions that were similar, with large crowds; the Coronation and the Silver Jubilee, and various major national occasions. All of them were special in their own way but our wedding was quite extraordinary as far as we were concerned.

'It made us both, and we have discussed it several times, extraordinarily proud to be British.'

He also spoke of the three-day tour of Wales, saying it had been 'overwhelming', and adding: 'All that was entirely due to the effect that my dear wife has had on everybody.'

The Princess had been very busy during the week that the announcement about her baby was made. On the Sunday, she'd been to a concert at Blenheim Palace and dined with the Duke and Duchess of Marlborough. On Monday, she'd gone to the National Film Theatre, and on Wednesday joined the Queen and other members of the royal family at the State Opening of Parliament. She'd looked stunning in a white fur coat over a white silk dress – the first Princess of Wales to attend the ceremony for seventy years. In the evening, she went to an exhibition at the Victoria and Albert Museum.

Soon she had to cancel engagements because she felt unwell in the mornings. However, she did go with Charles to the National Railway Museum at York and admitted that: 'No one told me I would feel like I did.' But she went ahead with the busy visit and was showered with presents for the baby – furry toys, ducks, bootees. It took two police cars to carry them all.

On 18 November, Diana appeared for the first time on her own at a function, when she arrived to switch on the Christmas lights in Regent's Street in London. Standing on a balcony above the street, she made a short speech. 'I know these lights give a great deal of pleasure to countless people in the weeks leading up to December 25, particularly to families who bring their children to see them.' She looked lovely and, like millions of other people, Charles watched at home on television as she switched on the lights.

Two days later, she flew by helicopter to visit her father at Althorp – her first trip home since before the wedding. The baby will be his second grandchild. Another daughter, Lady Jane Fellowes, has a little girl. For the Queen and Prince Philip, the baby will be their third grandchild – after Peter and Zara Philips, the children of Princess Anne and Captain Mark Phillips.

Towards the end of the year, the Queen became angry about the way the press seemed to be intruding into the private lives of Charles and Diana. The Princess was beginning to feel that she couldn't go anywhere, or do anything, without cameramen and their powerful telephoto lenses taking pictures of her.

She was upset when photos appeared in the papers of her dancing round the garden at Highgrove and flinging her arms round Charles's neck. These were private moments, she felt, not to be shown to millions of people. The Queen called the editors of Fleet Street newspapers to the Palace and pointed out that the Princess should have more privacy, and that reporters and photographers would be welcome *only* on official occasions.

Diana came in for a lot of criticism from animal lovers when it was reported that she had joined a hunting party at Balmoral, and shot a stag. Not the kind of thing she would have done before her marriage to a man who enjoys hunting and shooting.

Even so, she was back in favour with animal protection groups after a much-reported row with Prince Charles during a Christmas 'shoot' on the moors at

Sandringham. 'I didn't want to come here in the first place,' she is said to have told him.

While the couple were staying at Sandringham for Christmas and New Year with the rest of the royal family, Diana tripped and fell down a staircase. Later, a spokesman said: 'Happily, the Princess was all right. She was seen by the local doctor and then by her own, who confirmed there was no cause for concern.'

During her pregnancy, the Princess has been helping with plans for the nurseries for her baby at both Highgrove and at Kensington Palace, where the couple have their London home. Though a nanny will be in charge, people who know Diana say she will want to play a big part in bringing up the new arrival.

Her tremendous interest in the welfare of children was underlined when it was announced that the Princess had agreed to become patron of the Royal School for the Blind, the Pre-School Playgroups Association and the Malcolm Sargent Cancer Fund for Children. She is also patron of the Welsh National Opera and president of the Albany, a community centre in Deptford.

14
Highgrove

'A distinguished Georgian house standing in superb parkland. Entrance hall, four principal reception rooms, domestic quarters, nine bedrooms, six bathrooms, nursery wing. Full central heating. Fine stable block. Easily maintained gardens. Lodge. Farm manager's house. Pair of farm cottages. Dairy unit and farm buildings. In all, about 347 acres.'

That was the advertisement which appeared in newspapers and magazines when Highgrove house at Doughton near Tetbury in Gloucestershire came up for sale in 1980. Princess Anne, who lives only eight miles away at Gatcombe Park, spotted the advertisement and as her brother, Prince Charles, was looking for a new home, she told him about it.

Charles loved the place as soon as he saw it, and experts guess he paid between £750,000 and £1,000,000 to become the new owner. It's ideally situated for him – only twelve miles from the M4 motorway which can take him either to London or to Wales, and in beautiful countryside with hunting, polo and racing all close at hand. Many of his friends, as well as his sister and her family, already lived close by.

At the time he bought Highgrove, Charles was just beginning his friendship with Diana. When he showed her the house, she loved it, too – and was able to have a say in the redecorating. The couple employed a top interior designer, Mr Dudley Poplak, who has now completed the job of refurbishing the house.

Work has not really started yet, though, on the gardens – and Charles is said to be a very keen gardener. Just before Christmas 1981, a line of young trees, a wedding present from a society called the Men of Trees, was planted which will help to hide Highgrove from the main road that runs past the front of the house.

Highgrove has a full-time cook, housekeeper and gardener, with other staff when they are needed. The cook is Rosanna Lloyd, thirty-four, from Monmouthshire, who got lots of praise from customers at the Wolfscastle Country Hotel near Haverfordwest in Dyfed, where she worked before. The proprietor, Mr Andrew Stirling, said he was sad to lose Rosanna – 'she is a very talented lady' – and thought that bread and butter pudding, one of Prince Charles's favourite desserts, would cause her no problems at all!

Highgrove is part of the tiny hamlet of Doughton, only three miles from the market town of Tetbury. In Saxon times, there was an Abbess Tetta living there, and she probably gave her name to the town. Nowadays, 4000 people live in Tetbury, a charming village with curving streets, open spaces and old stone buildings. It clings to a hill, and the magnificent spire of its church dominates the surrounding countryside.

If the Princess wanted to do her shopping locally, and especially if she's interested in antiques, she'd have lots of shops to choose from. There's even one which, coincidentally, is called Diana's! Tetbury has always been a popular stopping place for tourists visiting the Cotswolds, and now it's busier than ever because of its new-found royal connections.

The locals are very sad that Charles and Diana seem to have been put off from shopping in the town because of all the attention, especially from the press. It came to a head when Diana went into a Tetbury sweet shop and found she didn't have quite enough money to pay. An embarrassing moment for anyone, and she was very upset when it made headline news. 'People should just let them alone,' said the ladies behind the counter, 'and let them get on with their lives.'

Until that incident, Diana had popped into a number of local shops. One storekeeper said: 'She is even prettier in real life than she is in her photographs – she is quite lovely.'

At the Prince of Wales public house in Tetbury, they are still waiting for a visit from the man with the same name. You can see Highgrove from the pub – but, as yet, the name above the door is the nearest the regulars have got to their royal neighbour.

In the autumn of 1981, Tetbury was full of journalists and photographers, but they left after the request from the Queen that Charles and Diana should be given more privacy. However, the people of Tetbury expect another invasion – of tourists – in the summer, after the royal baby is born.

When in London, Charles and Diana will be living in Kensington Palace. Their apartments are in a wing of the palace that was badly damaged by a bomb during the Second World War. It's been repaired and restored, and designer Dudley Poplak is busy decorating the rooms – a dining room, several reception rooms, a master bedroom, two guest rooms and a nursery suite. Kensington Palace is a royal 'village', and among the neighbours are Princess Margaret, Prince and Princess Michael of Kent and the Duke and Duchess of Gloucester. Until their apartments are ready, Charles and Diana stay at Buckingham Palace when they visit London.

They hope to spend most of their time at Highgrove. It's there that they'll bring up their family, in the heart of the English countryside.

It was the Queen who began the process of bringing the royal family closer to the people by sending her children to school instead of having tutors, by allowing television to share some of the family's private moments and by walking about among the crowds.

Now, her eldest son has married a girl who, though from an old and titled family, was a modern, working teenager before she met the heir to the throne. He has been all that a modern prince should be – caring, dashing, amusing, forward-thinking. As they begin their life together, the future of the royal family seems to be in very good hands.

15
The Royal Baby

Complete this chart as you learn about the royal baby.

Day of birth

Place of birth

Time of birth

Sex

Weight

Eye colour

Hair colour

Names

Christening date

Godparents

First public appearance

16
My Memories

These pages are for you to write down your memories of the Royal Wedding and the birth of the royal baby. Keep the book in a safe place and you will be glad to have a record when you read through it years later.

Acknowledgements

Photographs provided by:

POPPERFOTO for numbers 1, 6, 8, 15, 20, 21, 22, 26 and 28

THE PRESS ASSOCIATION LTD for numbers 2, 3, 5, 7 and 32

CAMERA PRESS LTD for numbers 4, 9, 10, 12, 13, 14, 16, 17, 18, 19, 24, 25, 27, 29, 30 and 31

SOPHIE LANE for number 11

KEYSTONE PRESS AGENCY for number 23

Photograph of wedding group (no 27)

FRONT ROW, left to right: Edward van Cutsem, Clementine Hambro, Catherine Cameron, Sarah Jane Gaselee, Lord Nicholas Windsor (bridesmaids and pages).

SECOND ROW, left to right: Princess Anne, Princess Margaret, the Queen Mother, the Queen, India Hicks and Lady Sarah Armstrong-Jones (bridesmaids), the Hon. Mrs Shand Kydd (bride's mother), Earl Spencer (bride's father), Lady Sarah McCorquodale and Neil McCorquodale (bride's sister and brother-in-law).

BACK ROW, left to right: Captain Mark Phillips, Prince Andrew, Viscount Linley, Prince Philip, Prince Edward, the Prince and Princess of Wales, Ruth, Lady Fermoy (bride's grandmother), Lady Jane Fellowes (bride's sister), Viscount Althorp (bride's brother) and Robert Fellowes (bride's brother-in-law).